To Live with Grace and Dignity

Text and Photographs
by
Lydia Gans

LRP Publications
Horsham, Pennsylvania

LRP Publications

An Axon Group Company

Horsham, Pennsylvania 19044

Library of Congress Catalog Card Number 94-75105.

Printed on acid-free paper.

Manufactured in the United States of America.

First Edition.

99 98 97 96 95 94   6 5 4 3 2 1

To Laurie, Nina, Greg and Bart

$\mathcal{A}$cknowledgments

I would like to express my appreciation:

To the Attendant Services Access Coalition (ASAC) for their financial help, and to Todd Groves, Jonathan Gold and the other activist members of that organization for making it all possible;

To my friend Marianne Miller for her patient listening and helpful advice on everything from commas to contents;

To all the people whose pictures and stories are told in this book, for their openness and willingness to share their lives because they believe in the value of the project, and, especially;

To Ed Roberts for always being ready to give me moral support and encouragement to get the work published and out into the world.

Many, many loving thanks to all.

Contents

A sliver of morning light from between the drapes reflects off the wall into Jo's face. She squeezes her eyes shut, hoping for a few more minutes of sleep. But it's no use; she finds herself listening for the familiar getting-up noises from the neighboring apartments. She turns her head and with her mouth activates the switch which turns on the radio. The announcer says it's 7:15—time for Jo to be getting up if she is to make it to her 9:30 class. But by herself she cannot get up. A quadriplegic, she can move only her head and her left arm. At 7:18 she hears the key in the front door lock, her attendant Lyn arriving to help her get ready for the day.

Jo is slow to rouse, while Lyn is bustling and cheerful, but they have learned to accommodate each others' personalities. Jo has taught Lyn how to perform all the tasks that Jo requires for her personal care. Lyn transfers Jo to the shower chair (a wheelchair with a cut-out seat) and pushes it into the bathroom for the usual morning functions, then back onto the bed for range-of-motion exercises. Lyn gently stretches and manipulates Jo's limbs to prevent them from becoming painfully tight and twisted. Together they decide on the day's wardrobe, jewelry, and makeup. After Lyn has gotten Jo dressed and into her electric wheelchair, she prepares breakfast and feeds her. She also fixes some lunch and stashes it into the pack on the back of the chair along with the books and floppy disks that Jo will need later on in the day. A friend or fellow student will help Jo at school, and another attendant will take over the dinner and bedtime routines.

Our technologically sophisticated society offers people like Jo all sorts of wonderful equipment and gadgetry to enable them to get around and participate in the life of the community. But the key element which makes it possible for them to live independently, outside of institutions, is people, the attendants who will come to their homes every day without fail, on time, to help with the personal, intimate care of their bodies which they are unable to do for themselves.

What does it take for a person to engage in a job which is physically and emotionally demanding, involves awkward schedules and generally pays little more than minimum wage? What does it take for the employer, the person who is severely disabled, to trust and depend so completely on the attendants who provide these personal services? And what kind of relationship develops between two people who become so intimate and so interdependent?

Jason doesn't mind getting up before dawn. His personal routine of shower, shave, exercises, and breakfast of fruit and granola, carried out while around him it is still dark and quiet, allows him to ease his mind as well as his body gently into the day. He rides his bike to Herb's house where he performs a similar routine on Herb's paralyzed body. He sees the task of washing Herb's body as not too different from washing his own, except that with Herb he gets paid. The pay barely keeps him above poverty level, but he is satisfied that in earning it he does no harm to the Earth or to any living creature. And when he is finished, early in the afternoon, there are enough daylight hours to devote to his painting, an activity that also satisfies his soul.

Jo and Lyn, Jason and Herb are examples, not archetypes. People who are disabled and those who work as their attendants are as diverse as any random set of human beings. That is why this project has expanded from a magazine article into a book—there is an enormous variety in the experiences and attitudes, in the ways of relating both physically and emotionally, among the people I photographed and interviewed. And, while each of the individuals is separate and distinct, they spend a significant part of their lives as pairs, in a totally unique relationship which provides strength and sustenance to both. Looking at, and listening to, what this relationship is all about is what motivated and inspired this book.

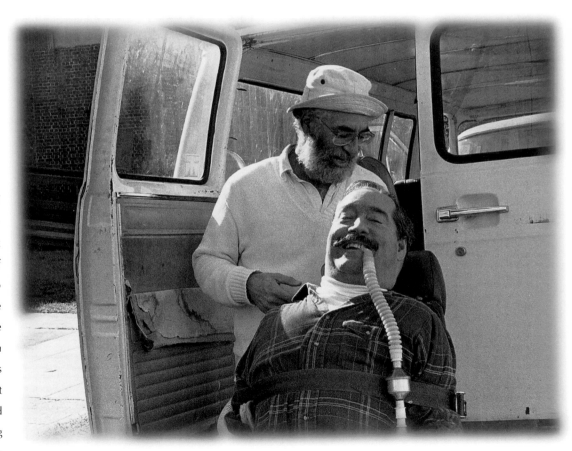

"I slept and dreamt that life was joy. I woke and saw that life was service. I acted, and behold, service was joy."

Jonathan Gold quotes these words of Rabindranath Tagore to explain some of his feelings about his work as an attendant. He talks about the concept of service, in particular the ideal of "selfless service." But, he points out, one cannot do disservice to oneself in the process, and like anyone else in the community, he needs to have an income to sustain himself. To do this it is essential for him to have a "right livelihood." To Jonathan this means his income must come from an "occupation that doesn't involve selling toxic chemicals to third world countries, on any level; doesn't involve lying to children, on any level; doesn't involve producing products that are totally useless and trying to get people to want them, on any level. It doesn't even involve passing on intellectual hierarchies, the established ideas of the tradition to young minds, which is what teaching is, on some level. It doesn't even involve that kind of guilt."

Jonathan gives a great deal of thought to conducting his life in harmony with his world and his ideals, and in the sense that attendant work com-

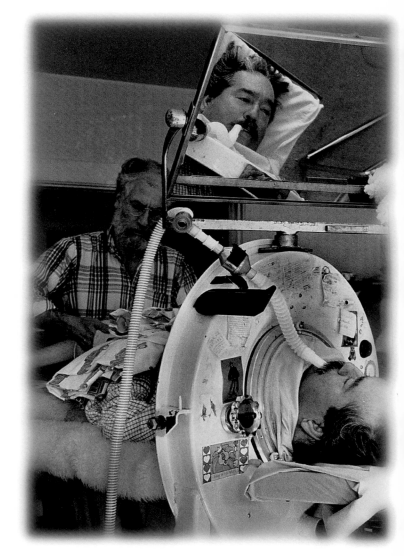

bines those qualities of selfless service and right livelihood it is, he says, "a perfect spiritual occupation."

He describes the work itself as "basically just working on a body," doing exactly the same things to another person's body that he does to his own. He begins to sound quite detached as he talks about being uninvolved, neutral about his clients' lifestyles (as long as they don't go out and do evil), how the client is just a body that needs to have its toes washed. But he is not as cold as this makes him sound; it is simply that he is very serious about doing a good job in taking care of another person's body, and that work is quite separate from his relationship with the mind, with the human being inside that body.

Ed Roberts is one of the people he works for; he has been working for Ed for many years. Trying to keep the detached relationship with him doesn't always work, he says. "Sometimes I forget our relationship. When I've taken him somewhere where he's giving a speech and I kind of doze off in the audience. And I suddenly realize, 'Wow, this guy's saying some tremendous things,' and it's Ed."

Ed Roberts is an eloquent public speaker, an accomplished organizer, a politically astute energizer of the Independent Living Movement who travels all over the world with his message. He was one of the founders of the first Center for Independent Living in Berkeley, serving for eight years as director of the California State Department of Rehabilitation. Then, with the help of a MacArthur Award, he went on to establish the World Institute on Disability. While Jonathan or one of his other attendants goes through the routine of feeding, washing, and grooming Ed, transferring him between the iron lung in which he sleeps and the wheelchair with portable respirator in which he gets around during the day, Ed gives directions, keeps up with the

ews and latest shows on TV, and carries on nvolved telephone conversations with colleagues, supporters, politicians, and potential unders of his many projects. All this is interpersed with bantering, silly jokes, and clever repartee. Ed and Jonathan can laugh at the world and at themselves. Even disability the subject of amusement. The problem with not being able to move is not being able to give the subtle visual cues that most people take for granted, such as pointing or turning one's head to look at an object of reference. For instance, there was the time Ed asked Jonathan to bring him "the file." Jonathan went to the bathroom and got the nail file. Ed meant the file of papers on the table in the opposite corner of the room.

Ed had polio when he was fourteen, and he quotes the doctor predicting that if he lived to adulthood he would be a vegetable. Now he likes to say, "The vegetables of the world are uniting! Watch out for those veggies!" He said it when "60 Minutes" did a segment on him. But all his activities and busyness are sometimes disconcerting to his attendants, and he is aware that he has to be sensitive to their feelings and their needs. He is prepared to listen and finds himself doing a lot of counseling and doesn't mind, he says, having an attendant who is dealing with some problems. Like most people, he has his friends and family, and his son Lee, who is the most important person in his life. Beyond that, his attendants are critical people in his day-to-day existence, giving him the freedom to live to the fullest and to participate in the life of the community.

While Ed easily says that his attendants often become his friends, Jonathan is more reticent and will plunge into a philosophical discussion of what friendship means. Does it mean wanting to do the same things? Ed likes to go to the A's games while Jonathan wouldn't dream of spending his time watching baseball. After mulling it over for a while, Jonathan agrees that they doubtless are friends since their basic attitudes toward life "probably are in harmony." More thought leads him to admit that there is a love between them which is "a spiritual thing," and for him the work itself is, ultimately, the expression of that love.

*C*aring and Sharing : Alana Theriault and Cheryl Wagner

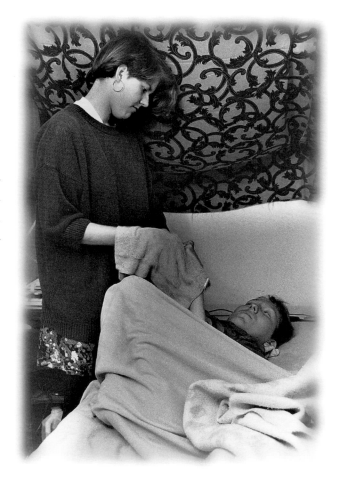

A lana Theriault—writer, poet, artist, student, activist—is physically fragile, weighing just forty-five pounds, but she is emotionally strong and has a wisdom and sensitivity far beyond her twenty-five years. She has had muscular dystrophy, a degenerative disease, all her life. Until she was fifteen she lived at home, where her mother and two younger siblings did her personal care. Alana felt they were all resentful and uncaring. Her absentee father did not participate in raising any of his children; he was "terrified," she says, of dealing with her disability. Her mother seemed tired, unhappy, not good at coping, and Alana bore the brunt of all her negative feelings. She recalls her mother as being angry over life's adversities and abusive to her daughter, who had to mask her own anguish, be grateful for what little she was given, and hide her feelings and her fear. Her mother, Alana declares, "had so much power over me—so much visible power."

At fifteen she went from a miserable family situation into a nursing home—"an awful place....It was terrifying being there. Everybody was waiting to die, including myself." Her social worker promised that there would be other young people in the home, she says bitterly, but there were only an eighteen-year-old boy who was comatose, a woman of twenty-six who was semi-comatose, and another of thirty-six who had had a stroke and couldn't speak. She shared a room with an Alzheimer victim. Alana made friends with some of the staff, but to them, she recalls, "I was a cute little girl who was different from the old people, but after they went home I didn't exist."

A bus took her to high school each day, and she tried to act like "your very typical sophomore high school kid." She admits now, "I went out a lot, I came home drunk a lot, I was stoned a lot, I cut school a lot," and the more he acted up the more restrictions the nursing home put on her. She "was very lonely."

After a year-and-a-half, she dropped out of high school and moved out of the home. A disabled woman-friend in Berkeley offered to share her apartment, and Alana engaged the county bureaucracy to obtain financial assistance. At first they treated her as a teenage runaway, but she appealed and ultimately won support. On her own for the first time, she had to learn how to hire, train, and use attendants. She had no concept of what to expect from an attendant or what her own responsibilities should be. She made many mistakes in the process—it was a hard way to grow up.

Once she settled in Berkeley, Alana began to explore diverse interests and develop her many talents. She wrote poetry and edited a publication of the work of disabled writers, became involved with a theater group called the "Wry Crips Disabled Womens' Theater Arts," and took Chinese language classes with the idea of applying for a fellowship to study rehabilitation practices in China. At present she is holding back from too many community activities in order to complete work on her B.A. at Mills College, with a major in creative writing and a minor in sociology. In her spare time she does art work—painting, drawing, collage—and her latest interest is in gardening, which she manages to do on the patio of her cluttered apartment.

Cheryl Wagner grew up in New Orleans in the midst of a large, comfortable family. She came to Berkeley at the age of twenty-one with a fresh degree in English from Tulane University. She immediately applied for a job as an attendant because a friend had recommended the work. It was not strange to her since she has a sister who is developmentally disabled for whom she has done basic personal care. Having decided to take a year off before starting graduate school, Cheryl wanted to "do something that involved interacting with people and was also beneficial," in terms of gaining work experience for herself as well as helping other people. Alana hired her because they "hit it off" and found that they share many common interests. Cheryl points out how important this is since they have to spend many hours together and are talking most of the time.

Cheryl has been working for Alana only as a substitute for the summer and is now starting an exciting new job teaching independent living skills to adults with developmental disabilities. Although being an attendant entails more responsibility than other jobs she has had, she finds that she is bored by the tedious, repetitive aspects. She is not fazed by the work itself, either doing intimate personal care such as cleaning up menstrual blood, adjusting

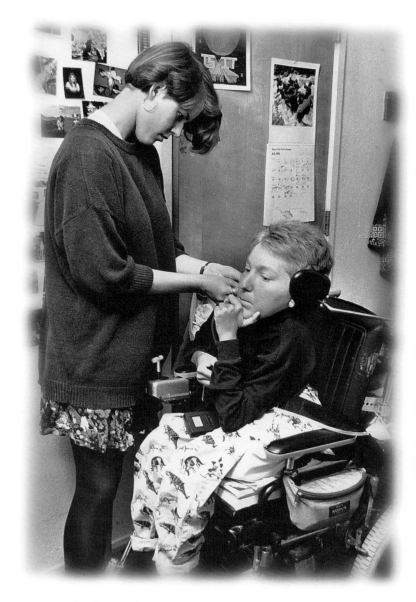

Alana's respirator, organizing her papers, or preparing vegetarian meals. She is matter-of-fact, outwardly directed rather than introspective, accepting of people and of life without agonizing over motivations or reasons.

Periodically Alana asks her, as she does all of her attendants, to evaluate her work and talk about how she feels. She poses "introspective questions" to which Cheryl admits she sometimes "makes up something philosophical" because she knows that Alana wants "more theoretical answers."

Knowing about Alana's abusive childhood, Cheryl understands her struggle for independence and the process of learning to manage her attendants. She sometimes feels uncomfortable because Alana is "always saying thanks whenever she asks for something" when it really is not necessary. Cheryl is just doing her job, but she realizes that this "is ingrained in her from the way she was brought up." Alana, struggling to preserve control over her own life, sees herself with her attendants in a business relationship in which she must establish her expectations of how the job is to be done: "It is important for my own self esteem to maintain that." She recognizes that otherwise she "slips back into that problem of them doing me a favor," which carries with it all the painful old feelings of helplessness and dependency, of wondering whether she was really worthy of being alive.

But a business relationship does not preclude friendship. Alana and Cheryl agree that once they are no longer forced to be together for two or three hours a day they will make time to see each other socially. Their common interests, appreciation, and understanding of each other serve as bonds that will grow between them.

$\mathscr{H}$elping the Flower Blossom: Annie Ewing and Angela Green

Annie Ewing was born with cerebral palsy seventy-four years ago in the small town of Durango, Colorado. There were no special schools or training facilities for disabled children in the community, so her parents cared for her. They owned a successful hardware business, and her mother would take her along to the store with her. It was a great treat for Annie, and although she couldn't talk she had a ready smile, and the customers loved her. Her father also took a large part in caring for her; she points to pictures in an old photograph album showing her riding around in a golf cart that he had outfitted especially for her.

Annie was in her forties when her father died. Shortly after that her mother became ill, so they moved in with a relative

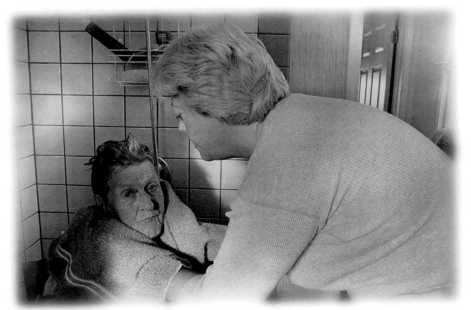

in Southern California. It was only three years ago that this relative could no longer manage being the caregiver, so Annie's younger brother brought her to Oakland, where he settled her into a large, comfortable house and hired attendants to care for her.

Annie is cheerful and cooperative, but she needs help with almost everything. Since she cannot talk, she communicates by pointing to objects or to written words, or she painstakingly writes out her thoughts on the typewriter.

Annie was not happy about moving to Oakland and having to leave her friends, but she has made new friends and travels often to visit the old ones. She loves to travel, staying in elegant hotels and eating at fine restau-

rants. She has season tickets for the symphony, opera, and several theaters.

All of these activities are shared with Angela Green, who has been her primary live-in attendant for the past two years. Angela has brought about great changes in Annie's life. Annie has always been treated, in Angela's words, "like the little flower in the chair, on a pedestal," never left alone, always protected by family as well as by lawyers and conservators. Under Angela's care this little flower has blossomed. Angela suggested an electric wheelchair. Family and conservator objected—it is dangerous and expensive, they said, and besides, attendants are paid to push her around. Angela herself was not sure that Annie could handle it, but she brought her to a wheelchair tore to get one and Annie took to it immediately. In no time at all she was maneuvering around the house and street and even crowded shops. Angela describes Annie's delight at her new, small bit of independence: "She can get the TV clicker and turn music on; she can get a Kleenex; she can go to the typewriter on her own; she can go to the garbage can and throw her Kleenex away."

For Angela, working for Annie and watching her move toward more independence has been an exhilarating experience. Angela studied nursing when she found herself in California, far from her native Alaska, divorced and with a small daughter to support. After she completed the Licensed Vocational Nurse (LVN) course, she worked in hospitals and clinics, and for the last fifteen years she has done private care nursing, though generally not as a live-in. Most of her cases were people who were physically deteriorating or terminally ill, and she could not allow herself to become attached to them. But with Annie it was different: "I adored her right away. She just sort of sneaks into your heart." Her love for Annie shows in everything she does for her.

Angela explains that Annie is different from young disabled activists of today who want independence and who reject the medical model in which they are considered patients and attendants are expected to be nurses or have formal nursing training. Because she grew up in an earlier era and because her parents had the time and the money to provide for her, Annie has always been totally dependent. When she is training the night-time and weekend attendants, Angela stresses that Annie is not to be alone, not to be held responsible for anything: "She does not have the same mobility or privacy or rights that many younger handicapped people have won for themselves." And Annie has completely absorbed the "institutionalized mentality: taking care of her caretakers, the feeling of being totally at their mercy, not wanting to anger them." It would be good if she were a little more forceful about letting her own wishes be known, Angela says, but on the other hand a good attendant should anticipate her needs and "smooth her life so that she doesn't have to work really hard to be telling me what she needs next."

Behaviors that are appropriate for an attendant are quite different from expectations in other kinds of relationships, according to Angela. It is important, she says, "that I pay enough attention or just somehow know that it's time for a drink…or it looks like this needs a little more salt on it because I know her and she wants more salt on certain things…or I just need to understand when we've been talking about a certain subject in a certain way…to make connections." With other people "you'd better go out and get some therapy

(for) second-guessing when some-one is too warm or too cold or might need to go to the bathroom before we go somewhere."

Angela is far more than Annie's caregiver. Besides going out to the theater and opera—new experiences for Angela — she in-volved Annie in the creation of an art project which won second prize in a local gallery competi-tion. It was an elaborate montage, using a clay figure that Annie had made in the cerebral palsy school that she attends four days a week, fancy beadwork that Angela does as a second occu-pation, and a collection of found objects. The title of the piece, which they conceived and executed together, was "A Few of the Many Lost." It repre-sented personal and environmental losses they had experienced—persons dear to them, animal species that had become extinct, human victims of the Holocaust. Both avidly collected the objects and worked late for many nights in Annie's garage as they created the piece.

Both women love traveling and have taken a number of trips in the two years they have been together. They have been to Hawaii, to Disneyland, to Las Vegas; they have toured Zion National Forest; and they are plan-ning to visit Annie's old friends in southern California. But a dream they have yet to work out is a trip to Angela's home in Alaska. It means flying to Fairbanks and then driving far out into the back country. Angela's cabin is three miles off the road, with no electricity except a generator, "way up on a hill with a fantastic view." It would mean a lot of work for her and finding extra people to help. But she knows that Annie would love it, and as far as she is concerned, that would make it all worthwhile.

Achieving Stability : Pamela Walker and Calvin Thompson

Pamela Walker needs assistance with personal care only on days when she doesn't feel strong enough to manage for herself, but she must have regular massage to relieve spasms and maintain tone in her polio-damaged muscles. Calvin Thompson's work for Pam involves performing massage and body work and helping with her stretching exercises, as well as doing household chores. They have been friends for a long time and are open and at ease with each other. They are both pleased that Calvin seems to have a talent for massage, and he talks enthusiastically about enrolling in a course to become a professional masseur.

Pam, forty-one years old, was born and raised in the Midwest, in a small town in Nebraska. She moved first to Oregon and then settled in Berkeley, "the first place I've ever been able to really be myself," she says. Because of all the support services and accessibility, she says she doesn't have to "put all my time and thinking into whether or not I can get somewhere, whether or not I can get help if I need it—so I can put the time and energy into doing the other things I want to do with my life….I am able to be a human for the first time in my life."

She is a political activist involved primarily "in the media aspect of disability images," monitoring and improving the image of individuals with dis-

abilities as presented in film and television. She has produced some acclaimed videos of disabled people in the arts and is a performer herself, doing, among other things, "sit-down comedy."

All her activities sap her limited energy, and having attendants who are dependable and responsive to her needs is crucial. Whether they are men or women doesn't matter to her; most important is being able to communicate really well, and being aware and sensitive to the fine line between the employer-employee relationship and friendship. With Calvin it works out. They "tease and flirt a lot, but we know there's this line—we both know," Pam says, "but sometimes we'll say, 'Oh well, maybe when we're fifty…,'" and this comment precipitates hearty laughter from them both.

Calvin's personal life seems a long way from being worked out. After a troubled childhood in a small town in North Carolina, he came to California about eighteen years ago, expecting "to make it big" as a musician. He spent years living in the streets, scrounging for food, working at odd jobs. It is difficult to get a coherent story of his life. His descriptions jump from one experience to another without chronological sequence and are interspersed with long digressions about people he has been involved with. From time to time Pam prompts him to get him back on track and organize his thoughts. His talk is animated and full of humor, but there is obviously much left out, things too painful to bring up in conversation. He is thirty-seven years old and has never had an adequate or steady enough income to make a home for himself. Most of the time he stays nights with one or another of the disabled clients he works for or friends he helps out, but there is no permanent arrangement. Longing to settle down and make a home for his two-year-old son, he pledges, "One of these days I'm going to get my act together. I want to really get my act together."

As different as their lifestyles and experiences are, Pam and Calvin have much that is intangible

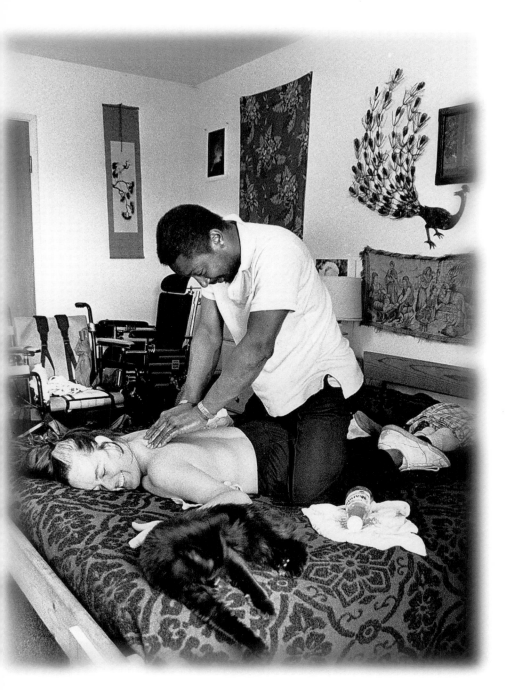

sensitive to other people's problems. There is no need to tell him to put things within reach of her wheelchair or not to leave obstructions in the middle of the floor. Her comments on this subject provoke his sense of the absurd, and he jokes, "I want these nuts cracked," as he pretends to put some nuts on the floor for her to roll over. He is a bit embarrassed by her praise. She is grateful to him for being "conscientious, always calling to check with people to see if they need anything." Since his living situation is so unstable, he cannot be reached by phone much of the time, but his attentiveness goes beyond the call of duty. Especially when she is sick, Pam says, he calls her regularly, even on days when he is not expected to work for her, just to find out if she needs his help.

Calvin has no problem expressing himself about his work: "I don't think I can get out of it. I don't want to get out of it." As for his feelings about Pam, his admiration for her is unbounded. "She's fantastic," he proclaims. "She's a remarkable person."

out important to give to each other. Pam provides purpose and stability in Calvin's life, and she lets him know how much she appreciates him. She recognizes that he has his own disabilities and that this makes him intuitively

13

At nineteen, Michael Butler was a confused youngster, hanging out in the streets with not much of a future. Orphaned at an early age, he stayed with an elderly aunt who could give him little guidance. They lived in a poor neighborhood beset by alcoholics and drug dealers, an environment which offered few positive alternatives. Now, just turned twenty-one, Michael talks with assurance and pride about responsibility and professionalism, about "taking care of business" and being able to "handle any kind of situation that comes up." Forty-three-year-old Ron Washington smiles proudly as he listens to him; Ron had a lot to do with changing the direction of Michael's life.

As Ron rolls along the street in his electric wheelchair going to and from work, he will stop to chat with the neighbors on the way. Quadriplegic as a result of an auto accident twenty years ago, he needs attendants to make it possible for him to live independently and hold down a job. Unfortunately, it is always difficult to find someone willing to come down to his rough South

Berkeley neighborhood. H[e] used to see Michael on th[e] street, and something about th[e] youngster appealed to him, s[o] Ron asked him if he wanted [a] job. Michael's first thought wa[s] "Me, work!" He says, "I reall[y] wasn't too much into working in those days." There wasn't much else to d[o] though, so he tried it.

Ron began to train him to do his personal care. "It felt pretty funny a[t] first," Michael confesses. "I never had to deal with touching another huma[n] being—you know the way you grow up these days, it was kind of weird!" [It] started out as a way to keep busy and off the street as well as make som[e] cash, but after a while he began to enjoy the work, and he discovered that h[e] was getting satisfaction from the process of helping somebody else.

As Ron trained Michael to take care of his body, he also taught him t[o] be sensitive to his state of mind, to listen and follow instructions without let[ting] his own ego get in the way, to be methodical and careful in everythin[g] he does. Ron has been hurt several times by careless attendants, as hav[e]

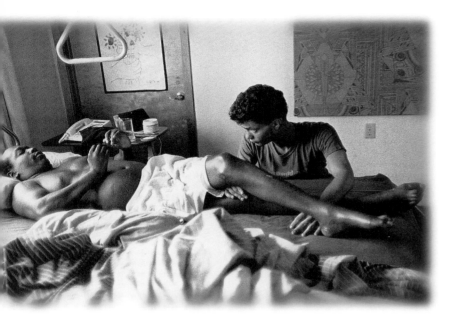

me of friends who are disabled, and this is an important issue for him.
here are also attendants who have suffered back injuries from improperly
ndling their employers. Michael talks about being aware of what he calls
ody dynamics," emphasizing that it works both ways. "Just like he would
worried about me doing something to him, Ron is worried about me."

But Ron and Michael's relationship goes far beyond worrying about the
reless infliction of physical pain. Ron is gregarious and thrives on being a
acher and mentor, a catalyst for bringing people together, stimulating
owth and change. With his outgoing personality he attracts people to him
herever he goes, talking to strangers, singing in his fine baritone voice, or
st "being outrageous." To shy, quiet Michael, he is a substitute for the
addy he never had, someone he has learned to trust and turn to for advice
nd guidance. When Michael talks about his plans for studying para-medi-
ne and physical therapy, Ron beams with pride.

Although Michael is only one of several attendants who work for him,
on cares deeply for him and clearly regards him as someone special among
e important people in his life. He has drawn Michael into his circle of
iends, exposed him to music and the arts, and encouraged him to explore
ew ideas and activities.

Now they are both making plans—Michael to sharpen his skills as a
caretaker of people's bodies, Ron to improve people's minds. Ron recently
retired from a job with the federal government and is thinking of becoming a
teacher in a poor, underserved community. Whatever they do, Michael and
Ron will continue to grow, both as individuals and together in their relationship—a relationship which clearly enhances the quality of both their lives.

When Debbie Fears first came to California from Ohio in 1978, she earned her living as a street entertainer—singing, dancing, and playing guitar and harmonica. She had her special locations: Fridays and Saturdays on Telegraph Avenue in Berkeley, and then at 18th and Castro in San Francisco. A three-hour gig would net her an average of $40 and a grand time to boot! The cold fog of approaching winter put a damper on that activity, however.

With her enormous energy and outgoing personality, it didn't take her long to make other connections. One of the regulars in her Berkeley audience was a disabled man who suggested she try attendant work and steered her to the Berkeley Center for Independent Living. She recalled that when she was in junior high school she had done volunteer work with youngsters who had cerebral palsy, and she was surprised and delighted to learn that people actually got paid for doing that kind of work. She has worked for a number of different people, but Mark Beckwith has been her main employer for the last ten years.

Mark left his hometown in Pennsylvania in 1978 to study at the University of California at Berkeley, which has long had an excellent Disabled Students' Program. Muscular dystrophy is slowly weakening his body but is in no way diminishing his determination to live his life fully, creatively, and—most important for him—independently. Get him started talk g about independent living, and he is eloquent. He decries a system that carcerates people without due process of law. "If disability is a crime," he says, "they should give a person a trial before they lock him up."

"Lock him up or give him the chair!" Debbie chimes in.

In a nursing home, Mark believes, there is no possibility of any kind of meaningful or useful life. He speculates, "What would the nurses say if a guy had his girlfriend come in there?" It's the difference "between life and existence." Besides, there is considerable evidence that disabled people can live independently in the community for a lot less money than it takes to keep them in an institution.

In-home personal assistance services are critical for indepen-

dent living, and this subject sets Mark off on another tirade about the system that allots disgracefully low pay for attendants and the bureaucracy that often deprives them of even that. The last time there was a budget crunch in California the attendants' paychecks were held up, and since most of these people live marginally already, this was enough to force some to quit and find other jobs. Debbie declares that she is fortunate to live in a rent-controlled apartment and that her children are grown up so she has only herself to support; otherwise she too would have had to find a different job.

It is easy for Debbie to list numerous reasons why she likes doing attendant work. She could be making a

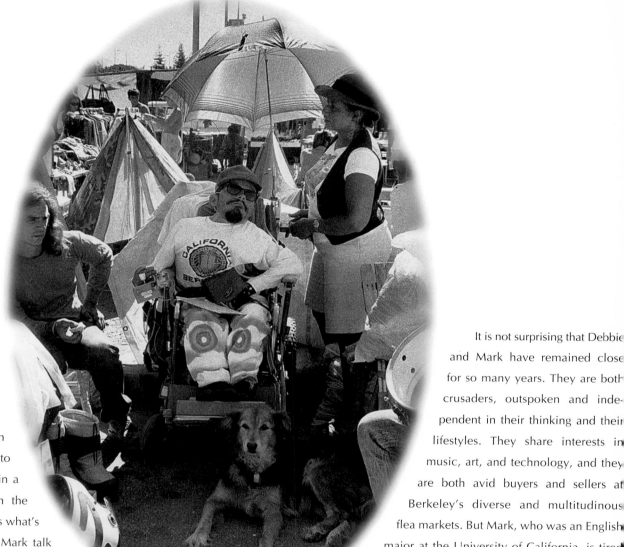

lot more money doing other work, but then she would be spending it on an extensive wardrobe, on a "hateful car eating up gas," and on a "shrink to help you deal with the stress." Working for Mark she can dress comfortably and ride her bike to work, and "have a great friendship in a relaxed atmosphere." They turn on the stereo and listen to music and discuss what's in the news—and it's fun. She and Mark talk about personal things, too, counselling and helping each other.

Mark agrees that he and Debbie are friends. He tells of being advised during his first orientation in the Disabled Students' Program that he should not get involved with attendants on a personal level, but rather keep the relationship strictly business. He doesn't see how it's possible to spend so much time together without developing strong feelings for each other.

It is not surprising that Debbie and Mark have remained close for so many years. They are both crusaders, outspoken and independent in their thinking and their lifestyles. They share interests in music, art, and technology, and they are both avid buyers and sellers at Berkeley's diverse and multitudinous flea markets. But Mark, who was an English major at the University of California, is tired of school and is now trying to establish himself in a marketing business which he calls *Cripton Enterprises*—and that is meant to be a play on words, he says—while Debbie is braving the academic world once more, studying for a degree in nursing. In whatever ways their lives might change, it is clear that these two want to continue for a long time, helping each other, listening to each other, and having a very good time together.

Struggling for Acceptance : Sue Hodges and Susan Haight

Sue Hodges is a woman of tremendous energy and wit, a crusader in the cause of access for people with disabilities, struggling for acceptance and understanding of the special circumstances that these people have to confront in their lives. But she has not always been so outgoing and articulate. She is forty-nine years old, but it has only been in the last eight years or so that she has been able to find her own spirit and humanity emerging from her personal battles with pain and increasing disability.

When she was a child and young adult, her approach to problems was to grit her teeth and carry on. It was important to her to prove that she could cope, to overcome the odds no matter how damaging to her spirit or her body. She reflects now that even when she was in "obscene pain" she held demanding jobs, determined "to be the best damn crip there was."

Over the years she changed in spite of herself. She did not find out until she was an adult that she had had polio when she was very young, something which her alcoholic mother had failed to tell her. This was recently confirmed by doctors and finally explained the physical problems she has had since childhood, and the fact that in spite of her struggle against pain and physical breakdown, possibly even because of it, she was experiencing increasing physical deterioration.

She met Susan Haight ten years ago through a "fat swim group" called the "The Maxi Mermaids"—a name they later changed to "Making Waves." Susan is thirteen years younger than Sue. On her first job, at a VA hospital, she found that she liked "sitting with people," being able to give care and comfort. After that there was a short stint in a nursing home, followed by a series of positions as a live-in attendant for people with disabilities. A back injury forced her into physically less stressful office work, and a job with an attorney got her interested in the law, so she went back to school. She recently graduated with honors as a paralegal. "That's different from being a paraplegic," she points out. Susan's quick humor has helped both her and Sue through some difficult times.

Five years ago they decided to live together. It was a decision not without conflict for Sue. Susan felt very protective of Sue and there was no question of their love for each other, but for Sue it also meant that she had to give up some of the independence she was tenaciously clinging to and accept the need for a live-in attendant. It has worked out because they have managed to develop a system for sharing most of the tasks of daily living. Though Sue needs a great deal more assistance with her physical care than Susan does, there are mental and emotional aspects of their lives in which their roles are

reversed and Sue can be the caregiver.

Sue continued to fight against her disability, although learning more about the causes of her condition and having Susan's support and understanding allowed her to be a little easier on herself as she went from using a cane to crutches to braces to a manual—and ultimately a power—wheelchair. She recalls that when she started to attend college eight years ago she asked the Department of Vocational Rehabilitation for a vehicle adapted for transporting her manual chair. Instead they offered her a power wheelchair and a van for transportation. Her immediate reaction was to refuse, determined as she was not to let them "make me more disabled than I am."

Sue has strong feelings about the "durable medical equipment" which is so essential to her daily functioning. She points out that the root of the word, "dur," means "hard." The equipment is indeed hard, she says. "It's unyielding and it's part of your life." Explaining that her crutches, braces, and wheelchairs are all extensions of her body, she objects to anyone else touching them. Seriously, but with a hint of whimsy too, she names every-

thing. Her crutches were Esperanza and Dolorosa; her newest van is named Annie Ankylosaur. She explains that Ankylosaurs were the dinosaur precursors to turtles, which are the female symbols of transportation and power, the mythical carriers of the Earth. This "personification helps, it softens the impact."

Sharing their lives with a menage of animals also has a mellowing effect, and there is a name and a story attached to each of them. Most important is Gallagher, Sue's service dog, who is trained to fetch and carry and be her guard and companion. A couple of other dogs and a collection of cats, domestic and feral, officially adopted and just hangers-on, are all part of the family.

After completing her associate's degree in junior college, Sue continued on to Mills College in Oakland. The small, attractive campus has pleas-

nt woodsy areas with meandering treams and charming old buildings—all of which are extremely difficult, if not mpossible, to negotiate in a wheelchair. At the same time she started there she got her first power chair. She and Susan, who accompanied her to school every day, explored the campus, finding entrances to buildings and restrooms that were accessible and paths that weren't impossibly bumpy with tree roots or dangerously sloped. They had some frightening experiences, and Sue recalls, "I really had to screw up my courage to do this. And I felt so stigmatized." The only other wheelchair-user was a slender young woman who wheeled around at high speed in her manual chair. She was "somebody who bought into 'disability cool,' made it look effortless…so we don't get stigmatized."

On campus she had "two majors, one that got me my degree and the other…that got me through the school. And they were equally full time." Students, faculty, and staff all needed to be convinced "that (a) it was OK for me to be there, (b) what I had was not catching, and (c) they could talk to me, and—I spent a lot of time with peoples' eyes sliding off me, and it's a very uncomfortable feeling." She persisted because she was determined to get the leadership training and the opportunity to develop her mind that she felt the college had to offer, and in 1989 she graduated with honors. She is grateful for Susan's constant support, which made it possible.

After graduation, Sue took jobs with local transportation agencies, working out programs to help people who are elderly or disabled make use of public transportation. But, just as she found at school, having a disability automatically means having two jobs, of which one is just surviving from day to day. And being a disabled person with a mission, as Sue is, means working even more than full time. She is constantly making speeches, organizing workshops, attending meetings to educate people to become more sensitive to disability issues. In an effort to streamline her work and ensure an income to supplement her meager Social Security benefits, she and Susan have launched a business called Disability Education and Advocacy Resources (D.E.A.R.) which runs training programs for people who serve a disabled population. They are discovering that being business partners represents new challenges to their relationship and their professional lives.

Sue is passionate in promoting causes she believes in, but in spite of her eloquence she has not always been so successful in inspiring others. It was Susan who taught her how to be political—to be tactful, patient, and sensitive to the people she wanted to influence. Susan has been active in politics since she was a teenager and understands how people and systems work. Over the years she has helped Sue learn how to get her message across. Sue says, "Susan taught me manners, she taught me humor...taught me how to carry myself in the world." But most important is being together, and being loved. They both have learned that "love is a softening, healing influence."

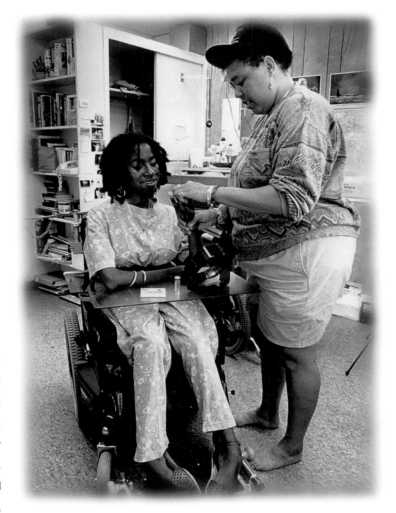

Michai Freeman is not yet twenty years old. She has had muscular dystrophy since she was eight, and has been using a wheelchair since the age of eleven. She grew up in Brooklyn with a supportive family and additional help from reliable attendant services provided by local agencies. Life in Brooklyn was "okay," but she "always wanted to come to California." Two years ago she entered the University of California at Berkeley and moved into a dormitory. Her mother came with her and stayed for eleven days, then left her on her own. The Disabled Students' Program screened potential attendants and made referrals, but Michai had to make her own hiring decisions and take responsibility for training and working with the people she hired.

The first realization that she was alone, she says, "freaked me out" for

a while, but she had no trouble managing. She has good intuition for whether a person will work out and says that she has generally hired her attendants on the spot, maintaining that "you can always tell if somebody is really a dork type." She admits she has been fortunate in that those referred have been "nice people," although in a pinch one summer she hired someone in spite of her negative feelings. Sounding very much like a Brooklyn native, she describes the person as "really lala-lulu, really strange!"

Majoring in women's studies with a specialty in Middle Eastern studies, Michai hopes to work for the United Nations or another international agency after she graduates. She chose a program that would allow her to take courses in a wide variety of disciplines, but her focus is definitely on

23

women's issues, a subject which, she says, "is very important to me right now. I want to improve the status of women." She has an international outlook and enjoys making connections with different types of people, taking great delight in the fact that in her two years in Berkeley she has had attendants of a wide diversity of ages, ethnicities and backgrounds.

Linda Atkinson is the only one of her attendants who shares her commitment to the Buddhist faith. They encourage each other in the practice of Buddhism and on most mornings take time to chant together. Linda, at thirty-six, has had many years of experience working with "people who have needs." She has worked as a drug counselor, helped prisoners plan for re-entry into the community, driven a van for senior citizens, and delivered meals-on-wheels. Eventually she got into tendant work, at first with the elderly and later with younger people. She has found this the most satisfying, though she declares that when it comes to a job, "There's not a whole lot I wouldn't do." She "wouldn't want to do housework for rich people" but would do it "for somebody who can't do it themselves."

But Linda has another passion that is drawing her in a new direction. Together with a group of friends, she is involved in a musical venture, composing and performing songs live and on recordings. Besides playing keyboards, she is engaged in learning both the technical and business aspects of producing records. With luck this will provide Linda a new career. Full of energy and creative impulses, she is ready to make a change.

Despite the difference in their ages and level of maturity, friendships are important in the lives of both women. Linda works as an attendant for several other people besides Michai, and they are all part of her circle of friends. For her these comradeships mean opportunities to gather together to share meals and conversation, for watching TV and rooting for favorite sports teams. Michai is quiet and studious and tends to be shy, but is like any young person in wishing for one or two intimate companions with whom she can share her thoughts and feelings about what is happening in her life. She reflects wistfully that an ideal friend would act the same way toward her as toward a non-disabled person but would be sensitive to her special situation. This means arranging transportation and going to places that are accessible to wheelchairs. A friend would be able to give occasional help when she's in a bind without putting her in a position where she is defined as a person who is helpless and needy. "I'd like a really buddy-buddy friend who'd come to my room just to say, 'How're you doing?'"

When she refers to her attendants, she also uses the word "friends," but in this context it reflects her attitude that the relationship should be one of mutual respect and a sense of responsibility to each other. It means that she regards them as people, not just a body or an object doing a job for her. On the other hand, while one might overlook certain faults in a friend, such as lateness or failure to show up when expected, these traits cannot be excused in attendants.

There are times when Michai acts spoiled and inconsiderate, times when Linda loses control of her temper and her patience, but in spite of their difficulties they remain friends. They spend time together outside of the work routine as their common interests and commitment to the practices of their Buddhist religion continue to forge a bond between them.

Bob Bruman has been working for Brett Estes full time for only a little over a year, but they both agree that the time spent together has been "intense." Their personalities, attitudes, and life experiences are in sharp contrast to each other, and there is a significant difference in their ages: Bob at thirty-nine is ten years older than Brett. Bob, outgoing and outspoken, will suddenly burst out with, "I really like this guy a lot, I tell you that. Really, I like him a lot." Brett is calm, soft-spoken, and reserved, wary about opening up to people or expressing his feelings.

Bob says of himself that he questions everything, is constantly searching, always learning. He has lived in many different parts of the world and has often made radical changes in his lifestyle and philosophical outlook, as well as his mode of dress and the eve color of his hair. As a southern Bap tist he worked wit Anita Bryant in Florid and ten years later h was a gay-rights activis in San Francisco. His interes and talent for art, however, hav been a part of him since childhood and he is now a successful artist. He had hi first show in San Francisco in 1985 and at this poin mounts several shows a year and obtains occasional lucrative private com missions. As an artist, he defines himself as a humanist because he paint portraits primarily. His vitality is reflected in his paintings, which are dra matically impressionistic in style and executed in brilliant colors. Hi impetuous personality shows on his arm in the scars from an attempted sui cide, and also in the fact that, if an opportunity happens to present itself, he likely to suddenly take off for someplace—Mexico, the South Seas, or anywhere someone invites him—for weeks or even months. On these occasions Brett will hire only temporary substitutes because he is confident that Bob will be back from any trip he might take. Bob gets deep satisfaction from his work as an attendant, and the stability that both this and his friendship with Brett brings into his life is very important to him.

Brett broke his neck in a water accident when he was six-

teen, on May 27, 1979—he will never forget the date. At twenty-two he moved to Berkeley, where he worked straight through to earn a master's degree in business from the University of California. After his graduation last year he got a full-time summer job as an intern with the California State Department of Water Resources in Sacramento. It was very hard for him to be working forty hours a week, having to get up at 5:30 in the morning, not sleeping much on account of the unaccustomed schedule as well as the heat. Bob was his full-time attendant for those nine weeks, and they agree that it was a "time of a lot of learning" for them both, a time of getting to know each other intimately; at the same time, each gained insights into his own handicaps and vulnerabilities. For Brett, it also meant for the first time seriously evaluating his career plans, thinking about how he wanted to live his life. Bob is encouraging him now to take some time out to find out what really interests him before jumping into the rat race for a traditional nine-to-five job.

Brett's personality is totally the opposite of Bob's, and the two men enjoy exploring and exploiting their differences, teasing and testing each other. Brett claims to be the one who is realistic; Bob insists that he is, too, but that Brett has his "own sense of realism." When Bob hears something about money, Brett says, he automatically has hundreds of thousands of dollars

going through his head and immediately starts thinking of how to spend them, while Brett is the one to say, "Wait a minute!"

They recall a recent encounter with a substitute attendant to whom Bob

took an intense dislike, immediately wanting to "punch him out" because of the way he talked to Brett. Brett defends the man, saying it was just his awkward manner and explaining that he just "doesn't have a good grip on life."

Brett is shy and reticent about making new friends, feeling most comfortable with other disabled people. He admits it is safer and easier being with those who really understand what it means to have to worry about all the things that dominate the existence of a person with a disability—whether the attendant will show up to get him out of bed in the morning, as well as concerns about getting his meals, being warm enough, having his wheelchair operating, and so on. Bob agrees that an able odied person cannot truly understand what it feels like but nevertheless insists that Brett has to get out of "this 'Crip Ghetto' concept of living. Real life," he points out, "is everybody." Brett tentatively acknowledges that Bob is helping him to expand his circle of friends as well as his outlook on life. Brett's problem, according to Bob, is that he is "from Modesto," where "they're still waving those flags…and not questioning anything." Brett insists that he is not politically conservative, "just cautious."

Brett and Bob are able to maintain the business part of their relationship and also be friends. Once or twice a week Bob "hangs out" with Brett after the two-hour morning routine is finished; at other times they might join friends for a barbecue. They estimate that they spend twenty-five to thirty hours a week together. They are very close and feel that they really understand each other. At the same time, when Bob is functioning as Brett's attendant, he is doing a job he takes pride in doing well. Brett expresses admiration for how quickly Bob learned the routine, and he lets Bob know how much he appreciates him. For Bob, that appreciation is one of the important rewards of the job. He tries to put into words the source of the deep sense of satisfaction he gets from his work, saying, "I find it good for my whole being to do this." It is not a matter of moral or spiritual values, but rather just "very enjoyable work. Sometimes I feel afraid, sometimes I feel tired, but it's a rare day that I feel resentment."

The serious tone soon gives way to more banter. Bob complains about Brett's grouchiness when he first wakes up. As Brett demurs, Bob says with heavy sarcasm, "Yeah, you were in a wonderful mood this morning," provoking Brett to point out that Bob "has the privilege of being the first one I see in the morning." Bob declares that by this time he has been up for quite a while and has enjoyed the early morning walk to Brett's house. "Now I know where you're at when you're fifteen minutes late in the morning—smelling the flowers," Brett scoffs.

Asked if he would recommend this work to others, Bob replies that he would—to the right person. Good attendants must be "looking for something beyond themselves." They have to enjoy working with people and have a strong sense of responsibility. "Besides," he says, his tone lightening, "if your quad gets rich, you might get paid real well some day!"

Actually, it's more likely that Bob will be the one to achieve economic success, in which case Brett will take over as his business manager. Brett's organizing skills, business training, thoughtfulness, and intellectual style are a perfect complement to Bob's impetuousness and sometimes unchanneled creative energies.

Lennis Jones and his attendant Thomas Tuthill are both very private men. Tom has worked for Lennis on and off for sixteen years, and they enjoy lively conversations on all manner of topics during their routine. They preserve their business relationship, however, and maintain an emotional distance, careful to respect each other's privacy and personal integrity. Thomas has had clients who he felt were "too interested," wanting to know "everything about my biz....It wasn't my people's way to tell everything." Lennis acknowledges that in hiring attendants he selects people he can relate to as he does to Tom "We just don't s around having hear to-heart talks."

When they finis their morning routine each goes off to h own occupation. Ler nis avers, "I will not as my attendants a per sonal question—I hav no reason for sharin their personal lives. But he goes on to say "Tom and I have know each other so long we know things, but even now we're not going to say what we know."

While they don't talk about subjects close to their hearts, it is easy to see that they are sensitive to each other's moods and aware of emotional a well as physical needs. Lennis can tell if Tom is having a bad day, and for those occasions they have compiled a set of priorities, listing things that absolutely have to be done and those that can be skipped on occasion. Still, Tom recalls the evening of the 1989 earthquake which rocked the San Francisco Bay Area when Lennis was among the first people he called to find out if his help was needed.

The attendant jobs suit Tom perfectly because they give him the time for his primary life work as a painter. His work has been hung in group shows, but he has yet to have his own gallery show. He keeps "getting complimentary rejection notes," but he is hopeful that he will find somebody willing to "take the risk of showing something a little different." Tom says that if it were not necessary for him to do attendant work to earn an income, he would do it as a volunteer because he believes strongly in trying to build "a more caring and less competitive society." And he talks about feeling humbled by the accomplishments of his friends with disabilities as he compares them to able-bodied people who spend their time "hanging out" and gossiping at Berkeley's ubiquitous cafes.

Unlike many disabled people, Lennis doesn't make a point of recognizing the anniversary of his accident. In fact, when asked, he is vague about when it happened. Nor will he dwell on the ten-year period he spent in the San Joaquin Valley Hospital, where his doctor proposed that a special wing be built on to house him. He was in his mid-twenties before he realized there was an alternative; once he was aware that there might be another possible lifestyle for him, however, he left "like someone would leave a burning building." He figured he could never be worse off "no matter what it was like on the outside." He lived for a time in his sister's garage and then in an apartment, but he was rarely able to go anywhere.

Then in 1972, when Lennis was twenty-seven, he heard about Berkeley and the Disabled Students' Program at the University of California. Lennis enrolled in the program, and life began to make sense again. He majored in psychology, a profession he had chosen way back in high school. Eventually he earned his Ph.D., and he is currently working toward his clinical psychologist's license, which means putting in many hours of volunteer counselling.

Living independently is not a philosophical issue for Lennis but "a matter of survival," and finding the right attendants is absolutely critical. He describes his first experiences in Fresno with one attendant who was incompetent and another who he calls a frightening psychopath. By contrast, he enthusiastically recalls his early days in Berkeley when there was a pool of attendants who were Vietnam War protesters who had chosen attendant work as alternate service. They were intelligent and conscientious about their work while at the same time pursuing other interests.

Later the political climate changed and government funding declined, forcing many social programs to be curtailed. By this time, though, the Independent Living Movement was gaining momentum (Lennis credits the Vietnam War with making possible the Independent Living Movement), and more and more disabled people were determined to live outside of institutions. Lennis points to those times as a model for attendant-client relationships. He and Tom reminisce about the 1977 demonstrations at the Federal Building, when disabled people protested program cuts and their attendants stayed close at hand to supply coffee and food or do on-the-spot wheelchair repairs.

Tom and Lennis are fortunate—they are particularly well suited to each other. Tom appreciates the opportunity to work on his painting and Lennis encourages that. Lennis, who puts a lot of energy into his work as a counselor, values Tom's reliability and efficiency. Each supports the other in those endeavors most important to giving value and meaning to their lives.

Hale Zukas is a familiar figure zipping around Berkley in his power wheelchair, which he controls with a stick attached to the helmet on his head. He is an activist and writer who has won several community awards. These days he describes himself, with great delight, as a comic strip hero. This came about recently when he found himself the subject of "Wee Pals," a comic strip in the local newspaper honoring people of achievement as role models for young people. Severely affected by cerebral palsy, he has great difficulty speaking, and his listeners have to concentrate to understand him. He will often spell out a word or point to the letter board he carries on his wheelchair tray. Since he is exceptionally bright, knowledgeable, and funny, it is well worth the effort to listen hard to figure out what he is saying.

Hale's friendship with Nina Sprecher goes back twelve years to when she was "pretty desperate, actually," with no money and no place to live, and he was looking for a dependable live-in attendant. He had recently moved into a pleasant, brand-new apartment that had a special appeal for Nina because it was near the Zen Center, which had become a focal point in her life. She has shared the apartment with him ever since, although she now works for him only if one of his other attendants fails to show up.

33

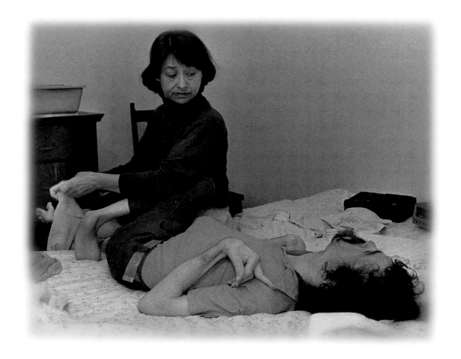

Nina was born in Poland, immigrated to the United States with her family when she was a child, and grew up in Detroit. After earning her bachelor's degree she moved to New York, immersing herself in modern dance and the theatrical life of the city. Somewhere along the way she got interested in macrobiotics, which led her to Colorado and ultimately to California to study acupuncture and Chinese medicine. Although she could not afford to complete the formal studies, she has absorbed many of the teachings and practices of Eastern philosophy into her way of life.

Hale's attitudes and interests are very different from Nina's. He is brilliant in mathematics, and his degree is in that field, but he also has a multitude of other interests, including meteorology and geography. Besides all that, Nina teases, he has a fantastic memory for phone numbers. He also studied Russian, motivated by an interest in the former Soviet Union and the possibility of employment doing technical translations. He once applied for a government job as a translator, and even had one article published back in the early Seventies, but he never got beyond that. "I guess that my subversive background did me in," he says ruefully, as he and Nina laugh at the very thought of him working for Ronald Reagan. He follows political developments avidly, and will write letters and participate in demonstrations on issues that concern him. He was one of the founders of the Center for Independent Living and worked there for ten years. Currently he is a researcher and policy analyst at the World Institute on Disability.

Nina, at fifty-four, is content to lead a quiet life, spending evenings at home and occasionally going off by herself to a retreat. Comparing herself and Hale, she says that they have "similar social consciousness and political orientations, but we need different living environments. I need lots of quiet. I like aesthetically pleasing, uncluttered, empty space." With a grin and a shrug, she asks, "So where do I live?" as she waves her arm around their shared living room with its jumble of books, magazines and papers, electronic equipment, maps tacked on the walls, and all the other effects of Hale's varied interests. Hale loves to travel, but that requires having an atten ant who can fit it into his or her work schedule. He has been advertising in the local paper for people to drive his van for short day trips with him.

Hale's family—he has a younger brother and sister—moved a number of times when he was growing up, he relates: "From L.A. to San Luis Obispo. We lived in three places in San Louis Obispo County, two of them on the second floor." His parents did his daily care when he was a youngster but began to hire attendants when he was in his twenties.

He was thirty-one when he moved out on his own. The move became possible when Congress passed legislation creating the Suplemental Security Income (SSI) program, which provides supplemental assistance for people who are poor, disabled, or elderly so they may have attendant help at home. Now forty-nine years old, Hale still finds that hiring and training new attendants is always "a drag. I just hate it." In the last few years while Nina was going to school, they looked for other attendants to take over his care. They have finally managed to cover his schedule, and Nina is pleased to be relieved of the responsibility and have the freedom to take the early morning walks she enjoys. She now has her degree in counseling and is looking for an internship to accumulate the hours she needs for a license.

It was attendant work that led Nina into the counseling field, in partic-ular "living with Hale and working out our differences." She discovered that, "Hey, this is interesting. People can talk and people can work out their differences. If we can do it, other people can do it." She realized that getting along is something that can be learned if people are motivated. "It's a choice," she says. "Getting along is a choice. And loving is a choice. It's not something that happens up in the sky. It's something you create. And of course it takes both people wanting to do it; one person cannot do it."

Nina is clearly a person who has made that choice. She is open about expressing her feelings and demanding that Hale interact with her—when he might prefer to ignore her and focus instead on the political situation or the state of the world.

Some day Nina will move out, maybe away to a place where the air is clean and there are wide open spaces. "I've talked about leaving ever since I moved in," she says, so they have tried to prepare for their eventual separation. But when asked about their relationship, Nina says without hesitation, "I love Hale," to which he responds somewhat more reticently, "The feeling is mutual." Hale is not one to talk about his feelings. He almost seems to take pride in being fierce and hard to get along with. Nina takes equal pride in getting past his tough manner. "He's not a guy to compliment

one," she points out. When he laments about her no longer doing any of his attendant work, she demands, "All right, let's hear it, Zukas," until he laughingly admits that he needs and appreciates her. For Nina, Hale is a friend and companion—someone she can feel free and open with, someone she can talk with about anything and know that he listens and cares. "It is wonderful," she reflects, "to be able to trust….I fully trust Hale."

Discovering Their Own Abilities : Liane Yasumoto and Charlotte Boettiger

Charlotte Boettiger thought that attendant work would "a good chance to get a feel for what a disabled person's is like," and would provide me useful background experience for the future, when she plans to study medicine. Now she says that the work is interesting and fun and means "doing something ally good, not just waiting tables." Best of all is the discovery in herself of ability to give and to take, to teach and to learn, to be a responsible employee and a sharing friend. Of course, working for Liane is easy, charlotte says, because Liane is a pretty special person.

Liane Yasumoto became a quadriplegic at the age of twenty when she broke her neck in an automobile accident. She spent six months in hospitals and rehabilitation facilities, then a couple more living in her church while family's San Francisco flat was converted for wheelchair access so she could move back in with her parents. It wasn't long before she decided to strike out on her own and applied for admission to the University of California at Berkeley.

Two-and-a-half years later, she looks back on that and other large steps she has taken and says that she never let herself or her parents think about it too much because then they would try to stop her, while she would refuse to listen to them, and there would only be conflict. So, she says, "I just kind of roll along...and then all of a sudden it all happens." She was surprised that first night in the dormitory at Berkeley, finding herself sleeping alone, not crying or even scared, and realizing suddenly that it was probably harder for her parents to let go than it was for her to break away.

Charlotte recently turned twenty-one, and she is finding that her parents are beginning to cut her loose, too. They have told her that they are going on a trip and don't expect her home for spring break. So she and Liane have a lot to talk about, many feelings and experiences to share. They talk about their parents, their high school years, their boyfriends—the whole complicated process of growing up and finding a place in the world. Liane observes

37

that they "really relate," and Charlotte agrees that "a lot of times one or the other of us will say something and we'll say 'Yeah, that really is true.'" Liane adds, "More often that not it's, 'Yeah, I've had that exact thought.'" And though Liane is the employer and, as Charlotte says, it is her job "to be Liane's arms...to get her the things she needs...to be careful...with the catheter...with transfers and lifting," they delight in their discovery of ho[w] much they have to give to each other, how each helps and supports the oth[er]

Liane exudes optimism and positive energy. Even after the accident s[he] refused to be depressed, despite nurses and counselors and social work[ers] insisting that that was a stage she had to go through. She accepted her d[?]

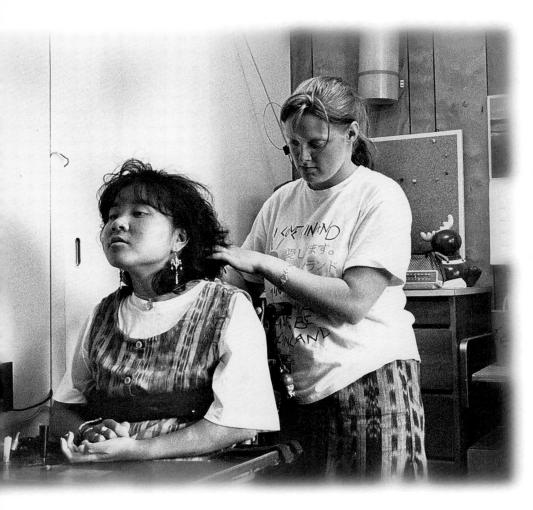

ity and moved on with life. Her spinal fracture was not total, so she
ld regain some function in her arms if she worked hard at it—and she
. She recalls thinking that there were three things she would really like
be able to do: one was using a hand-controlled wheelchair instead of a
n-controlled one, another was doing something "really practical like
atching my eyebrow or feeding myself", and the third was being able to
someone. She says she can now do two out of three—and is working
the hugs!

Because of all her accomplishments, Liane is often held up as a model for
er young people with disabilities, and she hates that; she hates being cast
"Super Wheelchair Woman" as much as she hates being pitied. She would
like to be treated as an ordinary person, and she
doesn't know how to deal with people who insist
she is someone special. Charlotte suggests that she
can simply say to them, "Yes, I'm proud of
myself," and then move on.

Charlotte doesn't want to "sound sappy," but
she admits that working for students with disabilities has taught her "to organize herself to study
and do well because they can do it with all their limitations." And she takes
pride in having a part in helping them organize their lives.

It does sound a bit sentimental, yet Liane hears the message. Since it
comes from Charlotte, she can accept it and appreciate its sincerity. She is
glad they can say this to each other. They say a great deal to each other, Liane
reflects—"We're both pretty chatty"—but it's not only idle chatter or specu-
lation about the latest episode of "Twin Peaks." They are both learning how
to communicate—to express their own feelings and to listen. The skills that
they are practicing in Liane's cluttered dormitory room will go with them as
they move out into a diverse world of people and places.

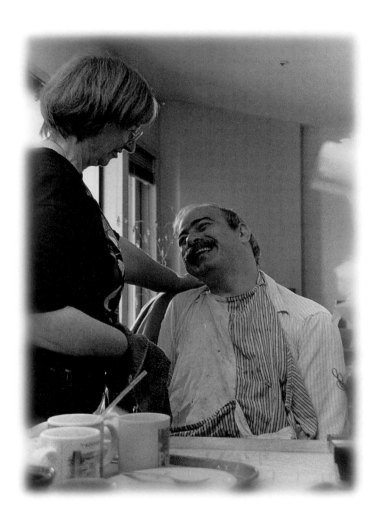

When Mary Fowler first went to work for Jim Gonsalves six years ago, she informed him that it would only be temporary while she looked for a full-time job. She often did attendant work in times of unemployment because the hours don't interfere with job hunting. Jim, who has cerebral palsy, agreed on condition that she give him two weeks' notice before quitting.

Some months later she found a good job where she could use her skills in mathematics and computer applications. She gave him notice, but by then things had changed between them. They had become sweethearts and had moved together into a new apartment. With both of them working, they were able to hire all the help they needed—morning and evening attendants and someone to clean the house. They bought a van with portable ramps for

Jim's wheelchair, and they now enj[...] outings on the weekends and a soc[...] life including his friends and he[...] Sometimes Mary's two-and-a-half-ye[...] old granddaughter stays with them.

Until he was thirty-seven, Jim liv[...] with his family, first in Castro Vall[...] then in the High Sierras, and finally [...] Bakersfield. It was a very lonely ex[...] tence for him. His mother gave h[...] very little personal care, encouragi[...] him to do things for himself. In ret[...] spect, he sees her attitude not as be[...] one of fostering independence b[...] rather of seeing his disability as a st[...] ma to be overcome or hidden. He spe[...] many hours every day grooming and feeding himself. Mary recalls him co[...] menting years later how much he enjoys having a hot meal, somethi[...] which most of us take for granted but which became possible for him on[...]

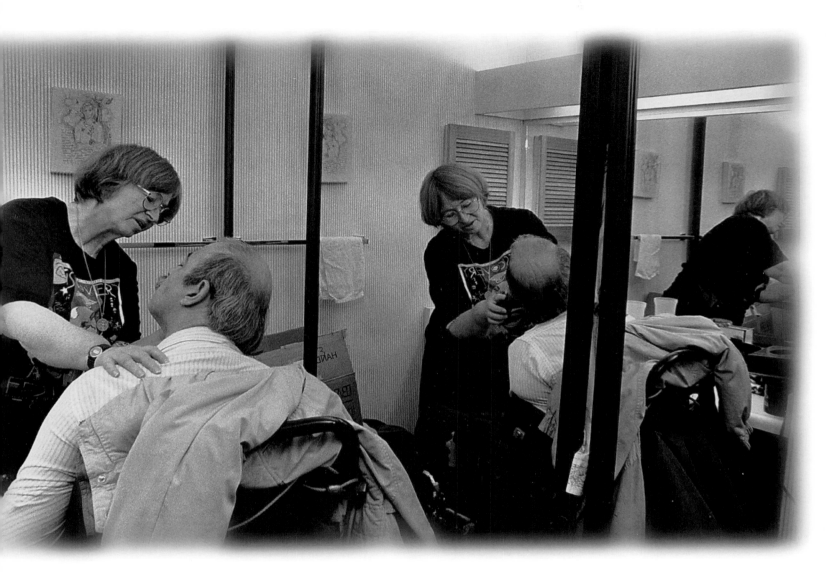

hen he had someone to feed him. In Bakersfield, with little access to out-
le stimulation, he developed hobbies, did an enormous amount of read-
g, and played chess by mail. At one point he kept forty games going simul-
neously. And he fantasized about going off and living on his own.

He moved out "cold turkey"—his first journey away from home. A
end drove him to Berkeley, where he was fortunate to find good atten-
nts. Being able to hire people to help him with all the personal care he

had been struggling for so long to do for himself was a new experience. That
was also when he got an electric wheelchair. Before that he had managed a
push chair by wheeling himself backwards, but now he could really move.

And move he did! He learned how to use the available public transportation and went daily to the Center for Independent Living, where he
worked as a volunteer on some of their projects. On weekends he would
spend the whole day in San Francisco. After so many years of being home-

bound, he wanted to spend every moment he could outside the house. He got a job at a center that administers programs for people with developmental disabilities and began to get involved in political actions on issues of concern to the disabled community. It wasn't easy, he says: "Believe me, when I first moved here everything under the sun happened to me. I was robbed three times, even on the way to a self-defense class….But for the first time in my life I was really living!"

Like many other people requiring personal care, Jim has had experience with an abusive attendant. He is not inclined to describe attendant abuse in detail but gives as an example one occasion when a live-in attendant neglected to leave the telephone within his reach at bedtime. Later, even though the attendant was nearby and was aware that Jim needed to make an urgent call, he refused to come and move the phone.

Jim goes on to point out that along with all the positive aspects of independent living "there comes the reality. And the reality is that things can't be perfect." He describes how, once he was on his own in Berkeley, he began to realize "that there were people all over the Avenue who were just as vulnerable…who were more psychologically disabled than I ever was."

Mary has her own concerns and experiences with disability. On July 1,

1987 she had a burst cerebral aneurism. It was followed by three brain op[er]ations and a long period of recovery. She can function quite well n[ow] except for lapses of memory and some confusion when she is in the mi[dst] of a lot of people and activity. She is troubled mainly by other peopl[e's] impatience with her and their failure to understand her problems.

Because of her situation, she feels a special sense of compassion [for] those with cognitive disability, which she believes is the worst thing that c[an] happen to a person because it is not visible. Besides, she notes, "All the n[ew] technological devices that are out there" are no good if "you can't think w[ell] enough to take care of yourself." On the other hand, people with physic[al] disabilities, such as those resulting from spinal cord injuries, "are kind of [an] elite, because they can almost pass for normal except that they sit down [all] the time."

Mary and Jim are both political activists, keeping intensely busy writi[ng,] demonstrating, campaigning, and organizing on behalf of citizens with d[is]abilities. For Jim this involvement started, Mary says, when he "got his fre[e]dom," that is, when he moved to Berkeley. Mary's experience goes back [to] the Fifties and Sixties in the peace and civil rights movements. With a deg[ree] in mathematics, she worked for various companies engaged in scienti[fic]

helpers, leaving Mary with a huge work load. But they are optimistic and full of ideas and plans. Jim talks about the possibility of forming a business which would advise public and private service providers on how to become more accessible. He would develop a set of standards and issue something similar to a Good Housekeeping Seal of Approval. He has also researched the possibility of opening up a restaurant specially designed for people with disabilities, with tables at the right height for wheelchairs, staff to feed people, and other similar features.

search and became active in the early campaigns to limit nuclear weapons sting. Then she became involved in fair housing and job issues in her neigh-rhood. Now she can apply the lessons learned in those activities to orga-zing in the disabled community. Her style is low key, her manner almost lf-effacing, her effect enormously persuasive.

Mary lost her job after she had the aneurism, and Jim is also presently unemployed. This means they cannot afford to hire attendants and household

Basically, they both want to do work that is in some way "disability related in a mainstream way." When times get better they will surely find something. Meanwhile, they have their home, their friends, and their love for each other.

❦

It doesn't take much time in conversation with Andy before one forgets the speech impediment that is one of the effects of his cerebral palsy. He has important things to say, and he can be very funny as well. Asked to introduce himself for the record, he recites as if he were providing census data, "Andrew Livsey, L-I-V-S-E-Y, forty years old, white, male."

As a child, Andy went to special schools where disabled children were segregated from the rest of society. There was always help from his family or from the staff of the institutions where he lived, so there was no incentive to learn to care for himself. Then in 1971 he went to college at the University of Illinois, which had one of the first programs for students with disabilities. The philosophy there was to encourage people to be independent by providing as little as possible in the way of personal care services.

For the first time in his life, at the age of twenty, Andy had to learn to take care of himself. It mean total change in his attitude, hav to overcome emotional as well physical barriers. "In institution he points out, "the more attenti you can get, the better." In c lege, "I had to learn to associ being independent with pow rather than with helplessness. was a real breakthrough for m He suggests, "You tend to associate being helped with being liked, w being cared for." People connect "being cared for physically with be cared for as a person."

After he graduated and moved to Berkeley, Andy had to make anotl change, but this one was considerably easier. Receiving financial assistar and then finding a part-time job put him in a position, for the first time in life, of being able to hire people and pay them to help him with his persc al care. This is the best situation, and it gives him "a lot more freedom" th he had ever had before.

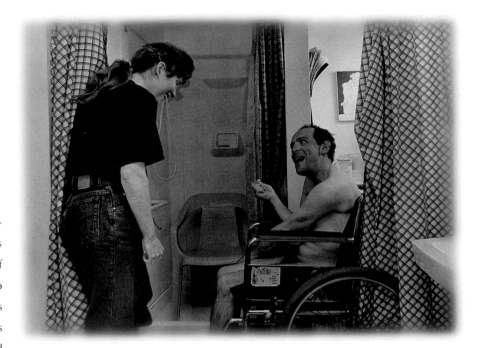

Andy lives in a three-bedroom house which he shares with two other people. One of them is Cindy Elder, who also works as his attendant. Cindy is only thirty-three, but her life has been far from easy. She has had two kidney transplants and must constantly monitor her health. Until she came to California five years ago she lived in Tennessee, where she had various jobs related to organ-transplant programs. She welcomed the opportunity to move to Berkeley with her boyfriend, but he died four years later and her "life kind of fell apart." She spent some time traveling, trying to get her "head back together" and decide what she wanted to do. Cindy reflects that for her, "It's very important that I do something meaningful," and attendant work satisfies that requirement. But because she expects that she will need health care soon, she will have to look for a position that provides health benefits.

In the meantime, working with Andy and other disabled people has helped her get some perspective on dealing with her own physical problems. She describes having to think about her condition, to watch her diet constantly and take medications that often have side effects, all of which, she says vehemently, "is something I just don't like!" She is well aware that "a transplant doesn't cure you; it just makes your life a little bit more normal." But she also realizes that hers is a disability which she can ignore from time to time, that she has the energy and strength for satisfying activities like hiking and riding her bike, and that she has many more options than other disabled people.

In the past few months since she started working for Andy, Cindy has come to appreciate his daily struggles. She recalls times when she was helpless and had to depend on other people and how she "hated that. I just despised that stuff!" Now she sees Andy and the other people she works for "finding their boundaries, limits, and accepting those to a point and then finding ways to go beyond them." She expresses admiration for them, but follows that with, "At the same time when I say that, I cringe." She declares

that she gets disgusted when people tell her how much they admire her for what she has been through.

Andy has developed a different perspective on this over the years. When someone says they admire people with disabilities, even if there is a tinge of pity implicit in that statement, maybe it is okay because, he suggests, "We really are, in a lot of ways, admirable people. I could have been a lot worse. Not that I'm ever what I could be; I'm also a hell of a lot more th I might have been." And, like Cindy, "There are times, believe it or n when I also forget … when I'm surprised and shocked by coming up agai something that I can't do." He goes on to admit to his own feelings abc other disabled people: "I do everything that other people do. I stare at pe ple. I say, 'Thank God I'm not like that.' And I also admire people when th ndle their disability in a way that seems, somehow—I want to say 'beau-lly.' I should say 'gracefully.' There is such a thing as grace in the way u handle your life. For all those reasons I think that some of us are mirable." After a pause he adds, "At least sometimes." Another pause. nd sometimes we're not."

Andy enjoys his part-time job at the junior college, where he tutors peo- with learning disabilities. He doesn't like bureaucratic duties or staff etings, but he gets tremendous satisfaction in working one-on-one or with all groups of students, proud that he is responsible for their learning mething. He also takes particular pleasure in the fact that this work puts in in the position of being a provider rather than a receiver of services. nd that feels real good—being able to give back to the community." rthermore, he says, "It makes me feel more like a grown-up." He is not king, because, in Andy's words, "Part of being an adult is working." It is o nice to have an answer for people "when they ask you innocently at a rty, 'And what do you do?'"

The majority of Andy's friends are not disabled, which he thinks is obably because he "was forced for years to be around disabled people most exclusively, and unfortunately I think that I associate disabled people with a certain part of my life that I would rather forget. And that's sad. That's really sad, but it's true."

He refers to his childhood spent in totally segregated schools. "Institutions," to him, "is an ugly word." He also recalls his experiences when he first came to Berkeley all by himself and moved into a building where there were a number of apartments "for crips and their hangers-on." It provided an "instant support network," but he soon found it boring and unproductive.

Another reason for associating with non-disabled people is purely prac-tical. He enjoys engaging in activities which he can't always manage on his own and going places that are not easily wheelchair-accessible, such as the beach or mountain trails. Cindy has her own interests and friends, but she and Andy often go places and have fun together.

For Cindy, the part of her life that she shares with Andy and their other housemate is somewhat like having a family, and it gives her much-needed emotional strength. Andy, mature and secure in his self-knowledge, is at a point in life where he can give to others a shoulder to cry on, a joke to laugh at, lots of good energy to live with.

Ethel Dunn declares smugly that she was fourteen when she first met Steven Dunn and decided, "That's for me." At the time they were students in a special school for children with cerebral palsy. Now he is sixty-three and she is almost sixty, and they have been married for thirty-five years.

Their accomplishments are impressive. They both have college degrees, Steve having earned a Phi Beta Kappa key and graduating cum laude with a Ph.D. in anthropology. Ethel's specialty in graduate school was Russian studies. Steve has had a number of interesting jobs as researcher, writer, and editor, but with the ebbing away of support for scholarly research it has become more and more difficult for them to support themselves. In 1969 they founded their own non-profit research corporation, which "wasn't hard to do," Ethel says, since "it was obvious that even personally we were non-profit." The primary activity of their venture is providing information and analyses on Russian and Eastern European issues for government and aca-

demic institutions.

Ethel and Steve b[oth] come from relatively well-[to-] do families who helped th[em] buy their modest but w[ell-] equipped home and provi[de] an income that allows the[m to] live independently, albeit [le-] gally, but makes them ineligible for government benefits. They have alw[ays] required help with personal care, Steve even more than Ethel, and th[eir] needs are increasing as they get older. They also have to employ people [to] do the various household chores. But it has been a lifelong struggle to f[ind] competent and dependable attendants, especially at the relatively [low] wages they are able to pay. They have had a constant stream of people, w[ith] few staying for very long.

One exception is sixty-six year old Tomy Maruyama, who has be[en] living and working with them for twelve years. He is one of the few sta[ble] elements in their lives, and they feel fortunate to have him. It is amusing [to] listen to them talk about themselves, about each other, and about their r[e-]

onship, and to note the mixed messages coming from all three of them. Tomy states bluntly that he really doesn't like this kind of work and will look for something else when he gets around to it, unless he decides to retire first. People originally advised him not to take this job, he says, at a time when he had many other options, yet he took it and stayed. Ethel avers that, "Temperamentally, he is not really suited for the job, yet he's an awfully good man to have around—there's almost nothing he can't do." In response to Ethel's comments that he is very good at his job, Tomy masks his pride by shrugging his shoulders and declaring that it just requires observation and common sense. Steve agrees that Tomy has no patience and no tenderness, but he attributes those traits to the Japanese culture rather than to his personality. One suspects that much of their complaining is a habit they have developed over the years of living together. There is no doubt that underneath it all, Tomy and the Dunns respect and care about each other.

Tomy comes out of two cultures; "Two different worlds," he says, "before the war, after the war." Born in Japan, he was in the United States with his parents when World War II was declared, and the family was sent to internment camps, first Manzanar and then Tule Lake. That was fifty years ago; Tomy was a boy of sixteen, yet he describes the experience as if it happened only recently. He recalls, "As we got in the train at the railroad station, there was a retired Chief Petty Officer, Nisei generation (American born of Japanese parents). He wore full uniform with all the medals as they took him to camp. A hero, had his picture in LIFE Magazine." Tomy is not political, nor is he one to brood over the past or the present, but the blatant racism behind that experience still rankles.

For many years Tomy had a management position in a large corporation, but the stress turned him into a "hard-core drinker," and twenty years ago he "just walked out," trying various less demanding occupations before going to work as an attendant for the Dunns. He has succeeded in staying sober since, and Ethel and Steve both praise that achievement.

Ethel talks about the difficulties they have had in finding and keeping attendants and household helpers. She says somewhat bitterly that all they really need is "someone who is literate, strong, trustworthy, brave, loyal—in other words, a grown-up person. And all of that for about ten thousand dollars a year plus a little food and a cot in the living room." She describes having to learn to act the role of employer, to insist that things be done as she directs and never to allow herself to be at the "mercy of her attendants." It took years for her to work through to the "conclusion that they're not family and I'm not their kid."

What makes it so hard, she says, is that, generally, "Disabled people don't have a very good self-image." She goes on to explain, "My parents loved me a lot and did a lot for me. But they still left me with the feeling that I couldn't really fend for myself and I really didn't know anything." Steve's experience was similar. In spite of all his accomplishments he was aware that his mother, until the end of her life, continued to believe that he couldn't manage his affairs.

It is the discussion about self-image of people with disabilities that leads Steve into the subject of the difference between those who have always been disabled and those who were accidentally injured. His image of himself is split into "two separate levels." His "head is accomplished," but on the other level, "Nothing works." He points out, "It's one thing to be disabled after having been able-bodied. You have some image, that is, if you have the courage and the strength to work back...and the world is supporting it too.

Whereas I—the way I am to me is normal, and the rest of you are strange and weird and have magical powers that I have no idea about." That he has some resentment about this shows in his agreement with a statement made by a social worker he once knew, referring to "kids who dove into an empty swimming pool at age seventeen, never having done a lick of work in their lives," and he feels that the militant Independent Living Movement is primarily of and for those kids.

Yet Steve is very political, explaining that he became a radical because of his disability. That happened in the late Sixties, "at the time when I ceased to be able to make a living from what I wanted to do." Although his father was intellectually a Socialist, Steve as a youngster was apolitical and had no sense of class identification. Now, he says, it is "the class of disabled that I identify with."

The Dunns and Tomy are all advancing into senior citizenship, but they remain mentally and physically fit. All three appear younger than their years. And they look as though they will continue as they are, Steve and Ethel involved with world affairs, Tomy working hard to stay in shape, employers and employee complaining gently but fondly about each other.

$\mathscr{P}$reserving Self-Esteem : Brian Hogan and Scott Ridings

"When you talk about disability getting in the way of being employed, that's economic, that goes to self-esteem. Eroding self-esteem and belittling people—creating a class of people who are ostracized. When your disability does that, you have to mobilize politically and become vocal. Enough is enough. Civil rights are for everyone. Democracy needs to come to everyone."

Brian Hogan speaks softly, gulping air between sentences because his breathing is controlled by a respirator, but he is eloquent and very convincing. Brian, spinal-cord-injured at sixteen when he was thrown from his ten-speed bike into a tree, is thirty-one years old. With a degree from UC Berkeley in natural resource economics and two years of law school behind him, he often finds himself engaged in political and social action. He has a creative side as well, with a love for theater and the arts. He is full of ideas for things he would like to write, and most recently found he has a talent for painting and is enthusiastically pursuing that. With this multitude of interests, Brian, in another time and place, might have been described as a Renaissance man. Now he has to focus on the mundane process of looking for a job.

Scott Ridings, Brian's attendant, is forty-three years old with a manner and appearance in sharp contrast to Brian's, yet their personalities seem to be in comfortable harmony. Scott has been an attendant for nine years, and he has found that it suits him well "because it forces me to not be so completely self-absorbed—to reach outside—and makes me a more complete person as a result." He has had other clients besides Brian over the years, and for the past year he has been spending three nights a week working for Last Call, a city of Berkeley program that provides emergency attendant services. In this job he is available to the entire disabled community. But he has worked for Brian for six years, and each thinks of the other as someone special in his life. Scott is rarely late, has never missed a day of work. He says that, unlike any other kind of job, "helping Brian in the morning fits into my emotional needs. It is a productive, life-affirming way to start a day."

Though their styles are very different—with Brian discoursing calmly and deliberately, Scott explosively and passionately—they find, as they discuss the day's news events, that they share similar opinions on most political issues. Also, both are involved with disability rights organizations and participate in activities furthering the cause of independent living. Scott had his own experience with attitudes about disability when he lost his index finger and part of his thumb in an industrial accident. He was shocked when

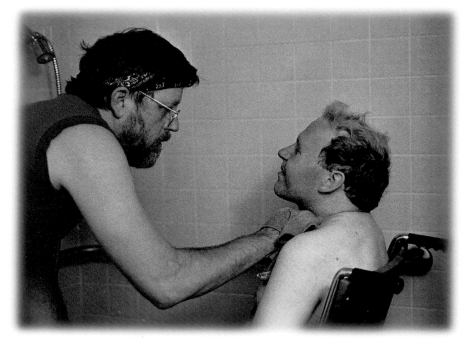

an insurance company representative referred to his case as that of "the amputee," and he found this a telling reflection of how society views the disabled. He is very cynical about the attitudes of able-bodied people and uses the words "malignant altruism" to describe the pose, "You've never seen anybody you didn't want to help." He is angry that in America today "people are very self-absorbed."

Brian is much less judgmental. He tells of his close personal relationship with a woman who had no prior experience with disability. Besides, he has other non-disabled friends who he feels can empathize even if they cannot understand all the "nuances of the disabled person's lifestyle."

Some of Scott's cynicism can be attributed to his experiences in working for Last Call, where he encounters many more "difficult" people on both the giving and receiving sides of attendant services. These people tend to be less competent in managing their lives, and Scott has learned to avoid getting emotionally involved with them.

Brian is concerned about small group of "disabled peop[le] who burn attendants out," an[d] wishes there were a way for th[e] community to regulate itself. H[e] would like to see people lear[n] that there are responsibilitie[s] that come with independent liv[ing] and recognize there is such a thing as abusive behavior toward attendant[s].

Both feel strongly that attendant work should be better rewarded an[d] respected as a profession. The subject of public attitudes toward attendant[s] causes Scott to recall his pique over a photograph of the two of them pub[lished in the glossy book "A Day in the Life of California," showing them[getting ready in the morning and giving Brian's name but not Scott's.

They talk about the difference between people who have had lifelong disabilities, such as cerebral palsy, and those who were injured in accidents[.] Scott characterizes "this intense sense of either 'The world is out to get me[' or 'The world is out to patronize me' from the guys who've had lifelong dis[abilities" as distinct from "the guys that have had it sort of as a break in life[

Many of them are able to keep going with that same kind of, 'Well, life is a bitch. Sometimes it deals you a weird hand.' They're more flexible while... the lifelong disabled can be real rigid." Brian agrees that there is a difference in their life experiences but stresses the importance of unity in political action, since they all face the same barriers.

He started working as an attendant to get out of feeling sorry for himself after his accident. He has never before stayed so long in one place or occupation. He is beginning to think about change, but this time it will be to enhance his skills and ability to serve the disabled community. He is reviewing his electronics knowledge in order to do wheelchair repairs, a task for which there is a critical need.

While Brian grew up in an average family with whom he is still in close contact, Scott was a military dependent and sees himself as "a reaction to ... being part of an authoritarian, militaristic structure." He describes his father as "sort of a martinet" and his mother as almost as rigid, so "these people always cracked the whip and I marched to my own drummer," which, he says, he is still doing.

Brian appreciates the importance of that and understands Scott's drive for a different challenge, yet he dreads the process of looking for a new regular attendant. Still, he knows that while he will eventually lose Scott as an attendant, it is very clear that he will never lose him as a friend.

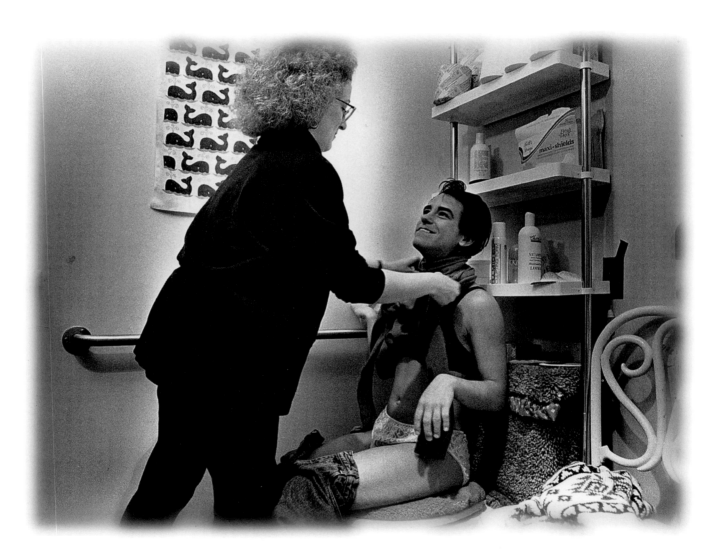

Carla Toth and her attendant Barbara Angle are both attractive, energetic young women, both holding down jobs and going to school, both caring about the world and about their friends. Carla is working on her B.S. in conservation and resource studies, while Barbara, who already has a B.A. in art, is now studying for a nursing degree. Carla is an editorial intern at *Sierra Magazine,* the sumptuous bimonthly magazine published by the Sierra Club. She receives no salary, but she is learning all aspects of an editor's work and meeting many people she would not otherwise meet. It is a job with a future.

Carla says, and it gives her her own identity outside of her small circle of fellow students and other people with disabilities.

Barbara migrated to California from New York after she finished college. It was difficult at first; she had no particular job skills, only the few things she carried in her backpack, and nobody she could turn to. She was twenty-one and very lonely, but she was

certain that she couldn't go back. She heard that the Center for Independent Living was looking for people to do attendant work and thought that was something she could do even though she had never before taken care of another person. It worked out, and she has been doing it with occasional breaks ever since.

Carla also knew she couldn't turn back once she had left home. Like many people born with cerebral palsy, she feels that she grew up getting mixed messages from her parents. She explains, "They didn't feel like I could live independently so they concentrated on how severe my disability was, but at the same time they wanted me to do everything for myself." By the time she was eighteen and a freshman at the University of California, she was desperately unhappy. Her parents had divorced and she was staying at her father's house, which wasn't even wheelchair-accessible, and commuting to school. She had no friends, she remembers; it was "no kind of life."

The decision to leave home was abrupt, spurred by her father, "scary, but liberating." Her life had been completely under her father's control, but once she left she could make her own decisions on how and where to spend her time and energy. For the first time she could hire attendants, and it was "very empowering to have a person that I could use, not in a bad way, but use any way I needed." She notes that although she is able to dress herself, it would take four or five times as long as it does with Barbara's help.

When she first started at the university, Carla did not do well. She registered for a full-time program, trying to be "like an AB (able-bodied person)." At the end of her first year, after coming close to being put on academic probation, she decided "something had to change." She enrolled in the interdisciplinary conservation resource studies major, which really suited her intellectual needs. She also decided to hire people to help her with personal care and domestic chores, but rejected assistance with her academic work. There were programs designed to provide help for disabled students, such as assistants to accompany the student to class to take notes if he or she has difficulty writing, but Carla found that unsatisfactory. "I used to hire note-takers only to have teachers relate to them instead of to me," she explains.

Doing everything for herself at school meant cutting down her schedule to only two classes each semester, but it is important to her to "be my own person." Emphasizing that "It's my study and not my attendants'," she makes it very clear that "I have no hangup with my personal care, but I don't want to relegate my intellectual life to a second party."

Usually Barbara comes on weekday mornings to help Carla wash and dress and to get her breakfast ready. From time to time she also does some of the cooking and household work, but it is not her favorite activity. She puts in a full forty-hour week doing attendant work, part of it in the Disabled Students' Program and the rest with four other people besides Carla. Barbara likes the variety, the intimate connections with people, the flexibility in organizing her time, the fact that it is not stressful, and, finally, that it is "rewarding…and a lot of fun." Now, after fifteen years, it is time to change and nursing is a logical profession to move into. It will be pleasant to earn more money and have the security of regular job benefits. But she expects that the friendships she has formed with the people she worked for will continue to be part of her life.

Before Barbara started working for Carla, each had heard good reports about the other, and when they met, they agree, they "got along right away." Since then their friendship has grown stronger, though they both have busy schedules with little free time for socializing. When they move into their new, different professional lives, the connection between them might become tenuous, but it surely will never be broken.

*B*uilding Futures : Michael Pachovas and Freeman Lancaster

n 1969, Michael Pachovas was serving with the Peace Corps in Ethiopia when he dove into a lake and broke his neck. The story goes that he hit his head on a submerged turtle. Michael doesn't know exactly what happened, but he says the friend who first told that story "was a Nixon supporter and had no sense of humor, so he wouldn't have made it up." He describes the aftermath: "You go from a place where you're about as independent as you can be, which is being twenty years old and living in the middle of Africa in your own little shack, (to) the next day with somebody having to put a toothbrush in your mouth in order to brush your teeth for you, and you have no sensation and no movement. That changes your perspective!"

Some people resign themselves to the role of helpless victim; some fight back and become tough; others find some alternative in between. No matter what the choice, Michael says, "Your outlook changes, you gain a lot of wisdom. And to be able to lead your life with some sense of dignity and grace when you have to be physically dependent on people is a really fine art that you have to develop."

One of the people he has depended on for the last twelve years is Freeman Lancaster. Freeman came from a small town in Louisiana, which provided him with only a minimal education and a strong desire to move to California. Michael is the only person he has ever done attendant work for, and for years he has done Michael's morning routine and then gone to a full-time janitorial job. He is not very specific about what originally motivated him, but he went to the Center for Independent Living to apply for a part-time job on the side, and they placed him with Michael. He does not read or write very well, so many jobs are closed to him, and he is unable to get a driver's license, but it has never interfered with his work for Michael. Recently he enrolled in an adult literacy program.

Freeman was in the National Guard when he was originally referred to Michael. The latter had misgivings about hiring him because he wasn't sure about having "a military person in my environment—I'm more of a pacifist." But Freeman had that all-important quality, "a good attitude," and also, as Michael describes it, "he exuded an air of confidence." Michael's trust in Freeman is well founded. He has proved to be capable and totally reliable; "invaluable" is the word Michael uses. He is grateful, too, knowing there are many disabled people who are neglected or abused by their attendants. He and Freeman have become friends, and when they happen to find themselves together with some free time they'll stop for a cup of coffee in a neighborhood cafe. On Sunday mornings their routine is stretched out over many hours while

they watch a ball game on television.

Michael's journey back from Ethiopia and into the mainstream has been a long one. Flown to Germany for surgery, he was lucky to be treated by a military doctor who prevented the paralysis from becoming more extensive. Then there were two years spent in a Chicago rehabilitation facility, which was "sort of like living in prison," where he had a constant battle to keep from succumbing to the "institutional mentality." At that time, in the early Seventies, there were only two alternatives: life in a nursing home, or life back in Crown Point, Indiana with his "large, rowdy Greek family who couldn't really deal with me." He chose Crown Point—at least, for the time being.

Two years of the family and he was ready to strike out on his own, to go to school, "away from Indiana—as far west as you could go without drowning." Four years later he graduated with honors in psychology from the University of California and went on to participate in a study of human sexuality at the university's medical center. He was in the first group of "sociosexual counselors/educators—that's a mouthful," specifically trained to develop expertise "in the interactio between disabilities and sexual function. He then became the sex therapist for county rehabilitation center.

He continued to work in a variety of coun seling settings, moving from one-on-one coun selor to program director to fund raiser, at which poin he realized that he could accomplish more as a polic maker, "which meant entering the political arena and really fight ing for social change." From being a "sort of plain vanilla liberal Democrat, he "became a hard-core political activist." Looking back, he recalls comin to a realization of the enormous difference between how he was treated a "an able-bodied white guy and as a disabled person. (It) made me angry made me want to fight back."

Forced to be practical, Michael considered starting a small business After taking some courses at a junior college, he became interested in rea estate and eventually got his broker's license. He is now working in a rea estate office and hopes to be earning enough money to support himself and his girlfriend, Shannon, when his Peace Corps benefits end in a few more

ears. He is still outspoken on political issues but has settled down to a more quiet life with Shannon and their collection of exotic birds and other pets.

Freeman's family is still in Louisiana, but his home is California, and Michael is an important part of his life there. Michael is someone he can always trust, someone special, giving him a kind of personal validation and support he never had before. He is not interested in working for anyone else.

Doing attendant work for Michael, he says, has been "part of showing I can get along with different people," and he enjoys his friends' reactions on meeting Michael when they exclaim, "Gosh he's big! How do you lift him up?" And when he runs into old friends around town who ask him, "You still work for that big fat guy?" Freeman smiles with pride.

From Companions to Friends : Concha Granados and Cuca Godinez

Cuca Godinez and Concha Granados have known each other for only a few months, but seeing them together one would guess they have been lifelong friends. Concha has worked hard all her life, but now, at eighty-seven, she has such painful arthritis that she is virtually homebound. Cuca is only sixty-five, and since her nine children have all grown up and her husband died four years ago, she says, she hasn't had enough to do. So she now works as a Senior Home Companion, spending several hours every day visiting and helping three elderly women. She is paid only for her expenses in connection with the work, but she considers it a regular job which she is responsible for and fulfills faithfully. It is Concha, however, that she spends the most time with and who has already become much more than a boss. "It's not just a job," Cuca says. "I think we're gonna end up like mother and daughter." Concha clarifies, "Giving the orders—I'm the momma."

For the last twenty-one years Concha has lived in a modest East Oakland apartment with her old friend, Philipe. He is a bit hard of hearing, and though he is kind and patient he doesn't talk very much, so Concha welcomes Cuca's company. Besides, it is much better to have a woman to talk with, Concha insists: "Men are men and women are women, that's all. They have ideas and we have ideas." And Cuca affirms with a Spanish saying to the effect that being different means they "don't cut with the same scissors. The conversation flows easily between English and Spanish. Both wome were born into traditional Mexican families and grew up moving ofte between Mexico and the United States.

Concha was born in Torreon, Mexico, went to school partly in Mexic and partly in Texas and, when she grew up, enrolled in cooking school El Paso. She learned American cooking and is especially proud of the fir pies she learned to make. It was a good trade to have, and she always ha jobs until she opened her own restaurant in Oakland, California. Althoug she has no children of her own, she raised ten nephews and nieces.

Cuca's parents came from Zacatecas, Mexico, and her family als moved often while she was growing up. After she married and began rai ing her family, she worked seasonally in the Del Monte cannery until finally closed in the Sixties. Now two of her children are still living wit her, but they are musicians who spend long hours practicing and mo nights working, so she has little of their company. Cuca knows what it fee like to be lonely. That is why she feels so sorry for one of her other clien who lives with a grandson who is always out. Cuca would like to help h find a place in a senior housing project because now, although she doesn

e alone, she is lonely.

Although they have lived in the United States most of their adult lives, both women have close ties Mexico—to friends and family ll there as well as to the old traditions. They compare notes on a host diseases and medical conditions r which there are home remedies anded down through generations of Mexican families. They recount experiences with cures using mixes of commonly found products or herbal teas, ures for illnesses American doctors were unable to treat: Mix cal (the lime at is used for tortillas) with vinegar for a growth; take lemon juice, glycerine, and three drops of iodine for a sore throat; avoid modern medicines, hich really are all drugs, and instead use traditional therapies and herbs rought from Mexico.

Cuca has been coming to Concha's house four days a week, originally ust to be a companion. Seeing that Concha never went out because her legs re very painful, she immediately decided she would try get her to walk again. But, Concha points out, "She think because she tell me—it's easy for me to do it." Now Cuca understands that it is just too hard for her friend to walk, but she can make her feel a great deal better by giving her daily leg massages, for which Concha is very grateful. They spend the rest of their time together talking, knitting, and playing cards. They laugh about the day they got so involved in a card game that they completely lost track of the time, forgetting to eat lunch and not realizing it until four o'clock. They have much to talk about, sharing a similar culture, attitudes, life experiences, and pleasure in each other's company.

Giving Dignity : Barbie Bentley

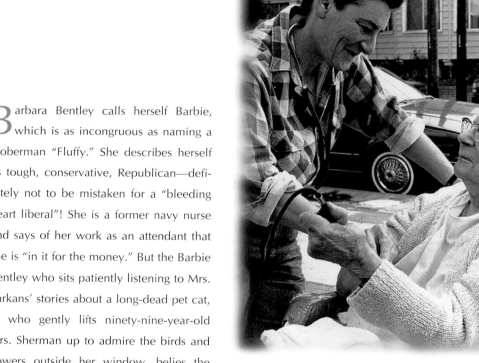

Barbara Bentley calls herself Barbie, which is as incongruous as naming a Doberman "Fluffy." She describes herself as tough, conservative, Republican—definitely not to be mistaken for a "bleeding heart liberal"! She is a former navy nurse and says of her work as an attendant that she is "in it for the money." But the Barbie Bentley who sits patiently listening to Mrs. Parkans' stories about a long-dead pet cat, or who gently lifts ninety-nine-year-old Mrs. Sherman up to admire the birds and flowers outside her window, belies the hard face she presents to those who don't know her.

On her way to Mrs. Parkans' house first thing in the morning, Barbie stops to pick up a McDonald's breakfast. It is what Mrs. Parkans wants, and Barbie serves it to her as if it were a room service meal in a modest but elegant hotel. Mrs. Parkans is the widow of a navy man and was independent and tough all her life. She is determined to continue living in her home

despite having had several strokes th[at] have increasingly limited her ability [to] take care of herself. Barbie washes an[d] dresses her and then transfers her int[o] her wheelchair while they talk about th[e] displays of photographs and knic[k] knacks that represent the important time[s] in Mrs. Parkans' life. Barbie rolls her ou[t] to the sidewalk in front of the house s[o] she can keep in touch with the neigh[-] bors. She encourages her to monitor he[r] own health as they check her blood pres[-] sure. Once Mrs. Parkans is set for th[e] day, Barbie has several more jobs to go to. She works hard to support her[-] self and her lover and a brand-new pick-up truck.

At Mrs. Sherman's house, Barbie makes her way through a jumble o[f] furniture stacked with papers, laundry, odds and ends, and piles of junk. Th[e] first thing she does is open the drapes and the windows to bring in light an[d] air. Mrs. Sherman is ninety-nine years old and somewhat senile. Her seventy[-]

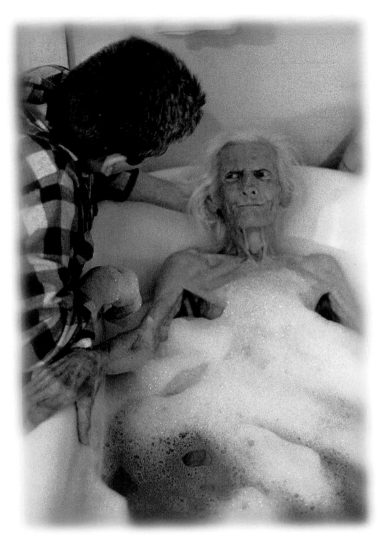

x-year-old son lives with her in a little cked-away house that, like its occuants, is a bit past its prime. He apolozes to Barbie for not being dressed and aving the house in order and offers her sandwich of dry bread and bologna. It obvious that this is routine, but Barbie ts him know she appreciates his oughtfulness in making her the sandich and avoids any mention of the

ess. She then proceeds to the formidable task of convincing Mrs. Sherman leave her bed and have a bath. It takes a long time and a lot of talking efore the old woman allows herself to be led into the bathroom, grumbling ll the way about having to pay Barbie "five dollars an hour to be made to o something I don't even want to do!" But Barbie never loses patience— ven though Mrs. Sherman is so light and frail that she could easily have een carried in and out in half the time.

Barbie now works mostly with elderly people. She says, "It's about ringing them a quality of life that they want and deserve, bringing them

close to normality, giving them dignity." That is why she has Mrs. Parkans call and wake her up in the mornings and lets her know she depends on her for that. She likes to work with these people because they accept her looks and her lifestyle. The key word is "bonding," she says. "I'll work with anybody I can bond with." But before anyone can accuse her of being soft-hearted, she insists that she is first and foremost a businessperson. Asked her opinion about what kind of people work as attendants, she says, "You don't see normal people doing attendant work. Nurses aides don't work with the disabled. You can't work with them unless you've had your own trauma....You have to have a lot of passion."

Barbie has it all: the passion, the gentleness, and the patience that comes with deeply caring for the people she works for, and it shows through the tough front she puts up to the outside world.

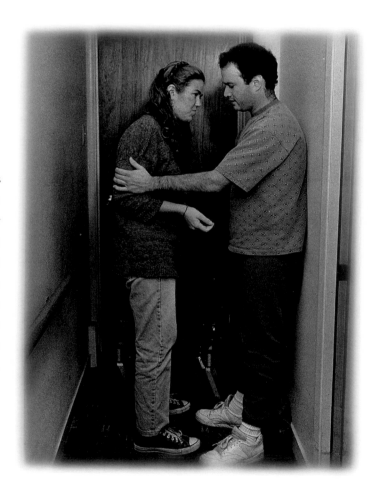

On March 26, 1989, Lisa Doble was traveling through Arizona with some friends. It was spring vacation of her first year at the University of California at Santa Cruz. She had unhooked her seat belt and gone to sleep in the back of the van. When the accident happened, she was thrown out the window and landed on her head. "They told my parents I was going to die," she says. "When I didn't die, they said I would never walk or talk again."

Two years and a number of rehabilitation centers later, Lisa returned home to the small apartment her parents fixed up for her in the lower part of their house. She uses a wheelchair but is working on relearning to walk. She talks slowly and with difficulty, but she makes herself understood. She is back in school, taking classes at a junior college. She swims regularly, participates in a support group for people with brain injuries, and plans to sign up for courses in weight training and yoga. She has come a long way in overcoming her disabilities, but there is much to learn and she still needs help.

Help comes from John Fingarson, her live-in attendant, helper, driver, therapist, teacher, and friend. John is five years older than Lisa and, like her, has lived most of his life in northern California. He has already been engaged in a variety of occupations, working as a disc jockey and a reporter, training as a baseball umpire and dabbling in local politics. Bored with a job he had "in retail," he looked in the paper one day and saw a help-wanted ad that "sounded interesting." The position was for a "life skills trainer" in a rehabilitation center that turned out to be only a few blocks from his home. Lisa came there as a patient at about the same time he started working, and they soon became friends. Five months later

'This is the best job anyone can have,' and some days it's, 'Why am I even doing this?'"

he was ready to be discharged with the proviso that she have a home attendant. She asked John—and they both have adapted well to the arrangement.

Lisa uses a wheelchair, but judging by how much progress she has made since her accident and how hard she works at her physical therapy, she might learn to get around with a walker or with canes. John works with her in daily exercises to help her gain balance and strength. He also helps her with small tasks that she can't manage and reminds her to do the things that are necessary to carry on with life as an independent person. John explains, "Persons with head injuries have a hard time following through, have a hard time remembering and a hard time initiating doing things." Lisa agrees, but then she laughs when he goes on to say that some people also have difficult behavior problems. She is basically a cheerful and cooperative person; however, she admits that she did have emotional problems to begin with but stresses that she had counseling help with that before she and John met.

John came into attendant work by accident and plans to move on to something else eventually, but in the meantime he is enjoying it even though at times it can become very frustrating. Some days," he declares, "are, like,

Hands on hips, he assumes a schoolmasterish manner and complains about Lisa not wanting to exercise or follow his instructions. She laughs, takes on a stubborn pose, but doesn't argue. John declares, "It wouldn't be a day when we don't get mad at each other at least once," but they have learned how to work out their disagreements. Asked how they deal with their problems, Lisa says, "We yell," which John promptly denies. He goes on to explain that they can tell each other how they feel, and then it's over with and they go on with the day's activities. Lisa points out that it is necessary to express anger, but she has had to learn to express it appropriately.

Lisa's goal is to be independent, to live by herself and to manage her own affairs. It is a struggle, but she has the support of a loving and understanding family. John will be moving on to new places and different activities. But for the time being, he and Lisa have a special relationship that goes beyond just working together on her physical rehabilitation. They are friends, and they are two young people learning to communicate their feelings, to listen, and to understand themselves and others.

❧

Sisters Living in the "Normal" World : Ivana and Ana Kirola

Most sisters will argue and complain about each other from time to time. They'll also stick together when it comes to confronting their parents, especially when the parents are immigrants who are putting much of their energy into making a living and trying to adapt to life in America.

Sixteen-year-old Ivana Kirola and her twenty-three-year-old sister Ana are no exception. In addition, they have a special bond: Ivana is legally blind and has cerebral palsy, and ever since she was three and Ana was ten, Ana has been her primary caregiver. Ivana insists she doesn't need much help because she wants to learn to become independent so she can move out on her own when she graduates from high school. Ana is in college now, and she too plans to move out as soon as she can afford to. In the meantime, she fusses about Ivana spilling juice when she tries to pour it for herself, to which Ivana will admit laughingly, "When it comes to food, I nee[d] help." Ana agrees, launching into a somewhat exa[g]gerated description of the great quantities of foo[d] her sister consumes.

The issue of how much help Ivana needs [and] wants is complicated. She would like to d[o] things for herself, but that takes too long, [so] sometimes she finds herself having to ask f[or] help. Ana will accuse her of getting lazy, the[n] praise her, acknowledging that "She's pret[ty] good about things." Ana really likes helpin[g] and, Ivana says, "Sometimes I can't get her [to] stop." At other times Ivana complains that An[a] treats her like she has no disabilities at all.

They describe their parents as workaholic[s] and their father, particularly, as not knowing ho[w] to deal with Ivana's disability. He will call for Ana t[o] come and help her sister on occasions when they bot[h] agree the help isn't needed—but they go through th[e]

notions just to satisfy him. Maybe he feels guilty, Ana conjectures, because he doesn't know how to help. Ivana expresses feelings of guilt about sacrifices her parents make for her, and Ana vehemently counters with, "You deserve it!" She goes on to explain that "it's natural" for parents to make sacrifices and to complain about their children.

Ana describes herself as an emotional extrovert who "really gets carried away" and will "talk about things—even to Dad," while Ivana is an introvert who keeps things to herself. Ivana worries about boring people, and again Ana scolds her for being so negative about herself and insists that she is too serious. Ana has a very active social life, and taking care of her sister does not seem to interfere with her many activities. She often invites Ivana to go out with her and her friends. But Ivana is at an age when she is not always appreciative of her big sister. As a junior in high school, Ivana feels that the worst thing that can happen is to be considered a "geek." There are a num-

ber of behaviors that she classifies as "geeky," including hanging out with her sister's friends and laughing too much.

Ana is majoring in psychology; she has always loved little children and hopes to find work with them. Ivana is considering a law career, but she is "having second thoughts because there are too many lawyers, and I want to be something that is really needed," possibly a social worker. With the help of a school aide who writes for her and describes things like chemistry experiments that are done in class, Ivana maintains a B average. She is having a little trouble with algebra right now, she confesses, but her mother has hired a tutor for her and she is working hard to catch up.

Ivana is ambivalent about whether she prefers to associate primarily with disabled young people or with "normal" people. She enjoys playing power soccer with other young people in wheelchairs, and she recalls occasions when she felt "sort of—I don't know how to say it nicely— proud, because all my friends playing soccer with me needed so much more help than I did." But she is cautious because, she says, "If you get too buried in the disabled clique, you don't know how to act in the normal world." On the other hand, she is sensitive to being teased by "normal kids about my habits, my rocking and stuff." Her feelings about her own disability fluctuate between a wistful "I wish I could see, I wish I could walk" to pride in competing in the world of "normal" people. Ana poses a counterpoint to Ivana's negative suggestions. "You are normal," she insists. "The attitude makes the difference."

Ana freely expresses her pride in Ivana, asserting, "We challenge her a lot, and she's gotten far. She does well in school, she has a future, she has goals—and she's got that positive energy." Ivana doesn't know how to accept her sister's praise; she is probably afraid of being "geeky." They fall back into the typical sisters mode, complaining over who monopolizes the telephone or eats too much, playfully threatening to beat each other up. The gifts of love and support and trust they give each other don't really need to be talked about.

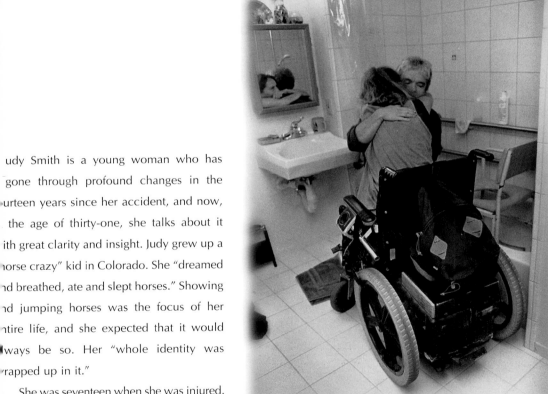

Judy Smith is a young woman who has gone through profound changes in the fourteen years since her accident, and now, at the age of thirty-one, she talks about it with great clarity and insight. Judy grew up a "horse crazy" kid in Colorado. She "dreamed and breathed, ate and slept horses." Showing and jumping horses was the focus of her entire life, and she expected that it would always be so. Her "whole identity was wrapped up in it."

She was seventeen when she was injured. She says, with no outward show of emotion, it was "a drunk driving accident. I was the driver, and I was the drunk."

Afterwards, when she was going through rehabilitation, she recalls that people encouraged her to go to college, use her brain to lead a successful life. "Shift your focus out of the body and into the head," she was told. "Don't try to use your body; succeed with your head." For a while Judy tried to follow that advice, starting out as an honor student at the University of Colorado, but she gradually lost interest. She needed time to find out who she was, to decide what to do with her life. People who knew her before she got hurt would say, "Oh, you're still the same person," but Judy insists that is a fiction. When you suddenly find yourself in the body of a quadriplegic, she asserts, "You're not the same person."

For the first six years after the accident she moved very little, either physically or psychologically. Attendants came twice a day to wash, dress, and transfer her between bed and wheelchair. Then she met Gail Cornwell, who had been studying and practicing what she calls "improvisational movement." Gail had only recently begun to encounter disability, first when a close friend was in a serious accident, and then when she herself began to experience movement limitations that come with aging. As she met other disabled people, people with spinal cord injuries who were using wheelchairs, she became convinced that "There was a real need to get out

of the chair and to explore being in this new body." She proposed to help them try, encouraging them to ask, "Can I get up on my knees? Can I roll around like we did when we were kids?....Can I reclaim that freedom?" It was the right question for Judy, who was ready "to figure out how to move this body." Now Judy needs help for only a few hours a week; she is studying martial arts and self-defense; and she is a member of the AXIS Dance Troupe, a group of disabled and non-disabled people staging performances all over the country.

Gail has always been an artist and a teacher. She also did carpentry and gardening and was proud of her skills and her physical strength. But in her early forties, symptoms of menopause and arthritis made her painfully aware of her body for the first time in her life. She embarked on an exploration of movement, looking at dance and the concept of improvisational movement. At the same time she made connections in the disabled community and began to do attendant work. At first she found little opportunity for experi-

menting with movement becaus[e] people's time and resources wer[e] limited to dealing with all th[e] immediate problems and eme[r]gencies of daily living. Then sh[e] met Judy, at a time when eac[h] was looking for what the othe[r] had to offer. In the eight years since, they have had an intense an[d] occasionally stormy relationship, have experienced profound changes i[n] how they conducted their lives, and helped each other gain in maturity an[d] self-awareness.

Gail is now devoting much of her time to caring for her mother, Blackie[,] who has Alzheimer's disease. She often takes Blackie along to Judy's house[,] where Blackie grooms the dog while Judy and Gail do their routine. On othe[r] occasions Judy participates in Blackie's care by taking her to the park, talk[]ing with her, or just spending time with her. To cope with Blackie's illness[,] Gail is changing her lifestyle, reordering her priorities, remodeling her hous[e,] and reorganizing her time to be able to provide for her mother. For Judy [it] represents another step ahead, going beyond independence from Gail into [a] osition of giving support and being able to help care for someone else.

Recalling their early days together, Gail now confesses to her queasi- ss at that time about doing the bowel program part of the personal care utine. She felt that way even though she had raised children, which she It gave her "a big edge on taking care of bodily functions and being com- rtable about it." Judy, hearing this for the first time, is surprised because e was sure that Gail was always "so okay with bodily stuff, and I was mor- ied by it." Gail points out that quite a few attendants have difficulty "tak- g care of ostomies and various other kinds of external...." Here she falters, d Judy fills in with, "Collection devices."

"Yeah, collection devices," Gail agrees, and they laugh at themselves.

A positive self-image, which is now generally recognized as an impor- nt requisite for a successful life, has been a struggle for Judy as it is for any people with disabilities. She reflects, "My self-esteem and my sense of ho I was in the world really began to change when I started reconnecting ith my body." Gail's movement work with her sparked that change, but eir relationship over the years has had a much more profound effect on dy's development. Being disabled and dependent on others for essential elp forces a person to either be "passive and nice" or be aggressive and

regarded as "an ingrate, bitter cripple." Midway between those two poles of behavior is "assertiveness," Judy says, and she has learned much of that from Gail. Being a strong person and almost a generation older than Judy, Gail could play the role of mentor, teaching her "to be direct...develop good communication skills," and encouraging her to become independent.

When Judy first moved in with Gail, she had never lived "alone" and needed help morning and evening, every day. Two years later she moved out into her own apartment. Now she has an attendant only three mornings a week, manages to take care of most of her needs on her own, and has start- ed driving her specially equipped van. All of this has come with "a gradual build-up of my own confidence and my own connection to what my physi- cal limitations are and what my physical potentials are." Her daily medita- tion practice, which she and Gail began together many years ago, is an important source of power and inspiration for her.

Both Judy and Gail are quick to point out that they were lucky to meet at a time when both were ready to experiment, to work and to learn togeth- er. Gail is not a magician, and Judy is not "Super Crip." Judy emphasizes, "Quality of life is a different thing for different people," as is the definition of personal independence. She knows some quadriplegics who will struggle with manual wheelchairs rather than give in and use a power chair. As for herself, she says, "I love being able to go fifteen miles an hour downtown." She has great admiration for Mark Wellman, the paraplegic who climbed Half Dome in Yosemite, and for the elderly lady with cerebral palsy "who went plowing through a field and fell out of her wheelchair and still came up smiling." It is a curious thing about disability, she points out, that "For some reason people think that in order to be happy you have to be cured or you have to be fixed."

Judy is happy. She says, "I love my life. I love the way I have my life set up." That is an enormous change from the angry, alienated young woman she was fourteen years ago, in a state of "shock and complete freak-out and not wanting to be in this body," and at the same time uninterested in focusing purely on a cerebral existence. Now she has her work, her independence, and friends and people she loves. Gail, on the other hand, is experiencing the beginning of a difficult phase of her life, having to deal with her own aging process and her mother's increasing helplessness. For her, the experiences with meditation and with improvisation in movement have taught her the value of "opening yourself to possibilities when...so many of them are closed."

The lessons that she and Judy have learned together and the solidity of their friendship will help them through and provide an example for other people struggling with the same kinds of problems.